WARNING!

This book contains highly combustible concepts that are intended to ignite a grassfire in your life, on your job, and with that idea you are developing. As you read these pages, be prepared for your Grassfire Effect to catch fire!

Pass this book on to a friend and receive a Free CD!

As I explain in chapter 9, one of the simplest demonstrations of the Grassfire Effect is what happens when you give this book to someone else. When you finish reading *The Grassfire Effect,* sign the space below and give it to a friend. Be sure to include a note about what you learned from reading the book.

Just for giving this book away, I'll send you a special Grassfire Effect bonus audio CD as my gift to you. (Even if you didn't buy the book, just read it and pass it on to a friend and I'll send you the CD.) See chapter 9 for details on how to receive your free CD.

NOTE: If you are the fourth person to read this book, be sure to return it to the originator of this Grassfire so he or she can see the Grassfire Effect in action!

This Grassfire was originated by:

Name/Address/City/State/Zip

_____

_____

_____

Comments: _____

_____

_____

_____

_____

Reader #2
(be sure to pass the book on, and then request your CD!)
Name/City/State

_____

_____

Comments: _____

_____

_____

_____

_____

Reader #3
(be sure to pass the book on, and then request your CD!)
Name/City/State

_____

_____

Comments: _____

_____

_____

_____

_____

Reader #4
(return the book to the originator, and then request your
CD!)
Name/City/State

_____

_____

Comments: _____

_____

_____

_____

_____

"When asked by a reporter what human character trait he most admired, Andre Agassi, after a victory at the NASDQ-100 tennis tournament, replied, "Empathy," the ability to see through the lens of someone else. If Steve Elliott, president of Grassfire.org, were asked that question, he would answer, "Creativity," the ability to change the world from one small spark of an idea to a grassfire effect that networks and creates economic and personal value. This book's overriding benefit is that it provides sensible structure to the creative process and the influence it can have. It is extremely well written, almost conversational in style, and gains real effect from Elliott's clear thinking, personal disclosures, and strong beliefs."

— *Arthur Trotman, President*
  Gevalia Kaffe Import Service, Kraft (retired)

"In *The Grassfire Effect,* Steve Elliott reveals the secrets for how an idea—though birthed as a tiny creative spark—can ignite a change front of personal transformation. Then, if nurtured and shared right, it can fan into a genuine grassfire, touching millions of people and the world for the better. The book is must-reading for anyone who wants to make a real difference—with their life, with their career or business, and with their faith. Buy an extra copy or two to give away to your friends or coworkers—and go start a blaze!"

— *Joel D. Tucciarone, CEO*
  Relational Marketing, Inc.

"I thought I knew it all till I read Steve Elliott's book *The Grassfire Effect.* It rekindled the energy of creativity within me. It will you too!"

— *Thomas J. Winninger*
  Author of *Bulls-eye,* Founder of Visionscope

"A life that counts, that has an impact, that makes a difference—all of us want that on some level. Well, how about a life that makes a significant difference, that has a maximum impact, that counts for both time and eternity? The difference between these two may well be found in *The Grassfire Effect*, Steve Elliott's forceful new book. But, be careful — it may not just change the world; it may change you!"

— *Frank Wright, Ph.D.*
President and CEO, National Religious Broadcasters

THE
GRASSFIRE
EFFECT

13-digit ISBN: 978-0-8054-4037-9
10-digit ISBN: 0-8054-4037-2

Published by Broadman & Holman Publishers,
Nashville, Tennessee

Dewey Decimal Classification: 153.8
Subject Headings: MOTIVATION \ CREATIVE THINKING
                    GENERATIONS—INFLUENCE

Unless noted otherwise, Scripture verses are from the Holman Christian
Standard Bible, © 1999, 2000, 2002, 2003 by Holman Bible Publishers,
Nashville, Tennessee; all rights reserved. Other versions quoted are the
Phillips, reprinted with permission of Macmillan Publishing Co., Inc.
from J. B. Phillips: The New Testament in Modern English, revised
edition, © J. B. Phillips 1958, 1960, 1972; and *The Message*, the New
Testament in Contemporary English, © 1993 by Eugene H. Peterson, pub-
lished by NavPress, Colorado Springs, Colo.

1 2 3 4 5 6 7 8 9 10 09 08 07 06 05

THE
GRASSFIRE
EFFECT

How One Small Spark
Can Change Your World

STEVE ELLIOTT

FOUNDER OF GRASSFIRE.ORG

BROADMAN
&HOLMAN
PUBLISHERS

NASHVILLE, TENNESSEE

This book is dedicated to
the more than two million Grassfire.org team members
across the country who have already experienced
the Grassfire Effect and are changing their world
one spark at a time.

And to my mom, June Elliott,
who has started more Grassfires than anyone I know.

Contents

Acknowledgments

One of the great wonders of life is how many people provide sparks of inspiration for each person's story. The Grassfire Effect is no different.

Bob and Randy Pritchard afforded me the privilege of using our shared story as the backdrop for explaining the Grassfire Effect. Without Bob and Randy, there simply is no story to tell.

Ron De Jong was among the first to field my musings about a book that would take the experience of Grassfire.org from the virtual world to the everyday world. Ron added much editorially to the content, especially the initial chapters.

Mike Jeffries, Lawrence Kimbrough, and Jim Barr believed in the Grassfire Effect enough to envision the book actually being published! Their prints are all over the manuscript.

Thanks to David Shepherd and the team at Broadman & Holman for seeing a spark in this idea, guiding me through the process, and exploring innovative ways to ignite a grassfire with this manuscript.

I'm grateful to Oscar, Becky, and our family at the Chesapeake Vineyard church for providing an incubator for my personal and professional development, as well as much of the content in these pages.

My children—Anna, Hope, Kirsten, Lauren, and Samuel—sacrificed time with Daddy so I could put my thoughts down on paper. Remember that I'm just breaking ground for you!

Above all, to my wife, Stacy, who has always stepped out on the water with me and has made this journey a "wonderful life" and a fabulous ride! All my love.

Introduction

Can You Picture It?

What do you see when you hear the word *grassfire?*

Does the word paint a picture in your mind's eye? The most powerful words in any language do just that—they create a meaning you can almost see, taste, touch, and feel. The dictionary definition becomes secondary to where the word takes you.

In my mind's eye, *grassfire* immediately creates a picture that carries me to the vast expanses of Texas, Oklahoma, Kansas, Nebraska, Iowa, and Colorado. I see a long, thin line of red-hot blades of grass stretching across the horizon, bending forward as if to reach out to the next untouched blade. I see that new blade being ignited in the blink of an eye and then stretching forward to reach yet another blade. And another. And another.

I also feel the wind. It whispers across the plains, bending the burning blades in any direction it chooses and sending the grassfire across the field like a mighty regiment that continually adds to its numbers until millions upon millions of blades have been taken in.

In its path, I see the blackened earth, scorched by the fast-moving grassfire but now cleared and made more fertile than ever before. And even though this grassfire stretches across my field of view, I know that somewhere, somehow, it all started with a simple spark.

Even the sound of the word *grassfire* carries me back to the American frontier, to the days of *Little House on the*

Prairie, Lewis and Clark, and the Oklahoma Sooners — to the thousands of brave souls who ventured to the gateway cities of Chicago or St. Louis and then went on to seek a plot of land so they could literally own a piece of history's greatest entrepreneurial adventure — the American dream.

Find Your Grassfire and Your Frontier

I imagine that many countries have trouble grasping the poetic power of grassfire. Europe, for example, lacks the vast expanses of frontier that still dominate the American landscape. Plus, in most cultures, an uncontrollable fire would likely be a bad thing. A danger. Something to be avoided at all costs. But here in America, we were birthed in the grassfire. We understand what liberty really looks like — millions of blades driven by an unseen wind.

A few years ago, I stumbled upon the word *grassfire,* and now it's the most important combination of letters in my daily life. I've been privileged to experience a real-life grassfire as the founder and president of Grassfire.org — one of the nation's largest online grassroots citizen-action organizations. The impact of this grassfire has reached the highest levels of government, spread across thousands of cities and towns, and touched more than one hundred countries and continues to chart an uncontrollable course. More than two million people have actively taken part in Grassfire.org's efforts to impact our culture and give citizens a voice in the issues of our day.

Charting Your Own Grassfire

In these pages I tell the story of Grassfire.org in hopes of inspiring your story and igniting a grassfire to spread across the fields of your life, expanding your influence to tens, then hundreds, then thousands, and even possibly millions of people. In these pages, you'll discover answers to the following questions:

- What is the Grassfire Effect?
- How do I discover my grassfire?
- How do I get my grassfire started?
- What will keep my grassfire going?
- How do grassfires grow exponentially, and will that happen to me?

After reading these pages, you'll look differently at every business, church, and organization you come into contact with. You'll no longer wonder why some businesses succeed while others fail. You'll want to get together with coworkers to "grassfire" a few ideas that can hopefully change your company and impact the world. And you'll discover the incredible power of a principle I call the Grassfire Effect.

In section 1, I take you step-by-step through the idea-to-reality process. It is my firm belief that each person was created to be a steady stream of potentially world-changing ideas. Also, there is a process for sorting through these ideas and seeing them become world-changing reality. In Grassfire terms, section 1 takes you through this entire process of igniting your own grassfire—what causes that initial spark of an idea and how that spark becomes a flame and then a wildfire.

In section 2, we'll explore how in life and business the Grassfire Effect can expand your influence, increase your profits, and infuse even the most ordinary days with meaning and purpose. Get ready: the Grassfire Effect is a revolutionary business concept that can grow your organization exponentially and can change the way you look at your world.

A Book That *Works!*

This book is unashamedly a motivational work and its goal is to rekindle the spark of creativity within you and encourage you to see your life as an ever-expanding grassfire that can impact generations. I hope you'll find inspiration with the turn of every page and that the principles of *The Grassfire Effect* will be applied to your life in practical ways. Let me encourage you to consider three areas of your life for application of the ideas in this book.

First, I hope this book will transform your thinking regarding your employment and help you start a grassfire right there at your workplace. Second, the Grassfire Effect can inspire you to launch new ideas and new endeavors and new dreams that could take your life in an entirely new direction. Third, it is my desire that this book will apply to your personal life; that you will see yourself as a spark that is setting ablaze a grassfire that will impact generations.

That's why at the end of each chapter you will find two sections designed to encourage you to apply the principles of the Grassfire Effect to your life. First, I list the "Key Effects" from the chapter—the primary points and principles. Next, I list a few "Fire Starters"—thought and discussion items that will help you practically apply these principles at your job, in the development of your new idea, and in your personal life. Consider *The Grassfire Effect* not as a workbook but as a *book* that *works!* Read this book with a pen in hand to highlight key points and write down the ideas that will literally pop in your mind as you turn the pages.

Read with a Friend

As you read this book, you will quickly discover that the success of your dreams and the power of your Grassfire Effect depends greatly on one key ingredient: other people. I contend that your dream will die and your Grassfire Effect will never change your world unless you invite other people into this process.

So read this book with another person. Get two copies and work through this book chapter-by-chapter with your spouse, a coworker, or a good friend. Be sure to find someone with whom you can trust your spark of an idea.

Don't Keep This Book!

Finally, consider a simple way to apply the principles of this book. When you finish reading *The Grassfire Effect*, give it away. Or get another copy for a friend or two. Passing this book on to a friend or coworker will reinforce the very principles of the book. Giving this book to a friend lets you test the principles of the Grassfire Effect right away. See for yourself what happens when a small spark (in this case, this book) catches fire with those around you. (Remember — I have a special gift for you just for giving this book away. See chap. 9.)

Most important of all, I trust that *The Grassfire Effect* will help you see with fresh eyes the potential world-changing impact of your life. Right now. Right where you are. Because whether or not you know it, deep within you resides a spark of a grassfire that can change your world.

That spark may be extremely dim right now. In fact, you may think the creative spark of your life has already been snuffed out by past failures. If so, keep reading and . . .

Get ready for that spark to come alive!

Get ready to risk again!

Get ready to explore your dreams!

Get ready to turn your dreams into reality!

Get ready to tap into the power of the Grassfire Effect!

Section 1

The Origins of Grassfires

KEY INSIGHTS AHEAD:

- *How is the world changed?*
- *Is world changing too big for you?*
- *What's the first step to changing your world?*

Chapter 1

Just One Idea

How the World Is Changed

Just one idea. That's all you need, Steve."

Think of all the conversations you have had in your life—tens of thousands every year. How many of them do you remember well enough to picture the setting, the face of the person you spoke with, the smallest details of the conversation?

I can still vividly recall the first time I heard those words: "Just one idea." I can see the window just over Jim's right shoulder. It was a sunny day. I was taking a quick break between classes to meet with Jim. But I certainly wasn't expecting anything extraordinary to happen. Then those words came: "Just one idea and you can change the world."

How the World Is Changed

The idea of changing the world was new to me. Well, not totally new. As a twenty-one-year-old college student,

I was attending a university that prided itself on developing world-changing leaders. Education is a privilege, we were told; world-changing leadership was our responsibility.

Yet this conversation with Jim was different. Jim wasn't talking about some implied obligation. This was about something more. This was about how the world actually gets changed. Period. End of story. Every day. By people like you and me.

Too Grand for You?

Changing the world sounds too grand a concept. In fact, it's so grand most people never even consider that they can possibly do such a thing. Instead, we leave the world changing to the superstars, the politicians, the scientists, the business leaders, and the media. We march through our little corner of life, hoping that the world's changes will not overrun us. We scan the papers, watch TV, and read books so we won't fall behind. *That's enough of a task,* we think. *Leave the world changing to others.*

And that's where we get off track. Distracted by the results of the world-changing process—the conclusion, the final chapter—we quickly get overwhelmed and fail to realize every world-changing event starts with a very small spark.

Remember when you were a child? What did you want to be? A teacher? A nurse? A fireman? Which dreams from your youth survived to adulthood? My point is this: Somewhere deep within each person's heart is a dream, something we want to become or accomplish or attain. As children, we dare to dream—the wilder, the better. But when we become adults, we seem to spend most of our days burying those dreams while we trudge through our routine.

Will You Dare to Dream Again?

I have a friend who has seen many of his "inventions" become successes. Unfortunately, he's not the one benefiting from them. He had the dreams but never did anything with them. Instead, someone else made his dream a reality and received the accompanying rewards.

Still, my friend can't escape his dreams. And neither can you because every so often something happens to awaken the dream and make it come alive again in colors so bright and vibrant it hurts your eyes. Usually, this happens when we are confronted with someone who has accomplished our dream. We see the finished product in someone else's life, and for only a moment the dream awakens.

But then, reality sets in, and we see a great chasm between them and us, between a dream fulfilled in someone else and the disappointment of where we are. To make ourselves feel better, we think, *He's just lucky* or *He's probably on his third marriage, and his kids don't know him.* Excuses aside, why can't you realize that dream? The answer is as clear and simple as the dreams of your childhood: You've lost sight of, or never understood, the vital first ingredient to changing the world and realizing dreams.

The World-Changing Riddle

"Just one idea. That's all you need, Steve. Just one idea and you can change the world."

I looked at Jim, partially puzzled. Somehow, I knew what he was saying was entirely true, yet my mind was processing his words as fast as possible and I couldn't solve the riddle. Then Jim began recounting the lives of some great people: Martin Luther King Jr., the apostle Paul, George Washington Carver. What did each man have in common? They took simple ideas and applied them to their world, and the world has never been the same.

Consider the story of George Washington Carver. Legend has it that he was walking through a field when he cried out, "Mr. Creator, show me the secrets of the universe!" God let him know quite clearly that little George couldn't handle such knowledge. "Little man, you ask for too much. Ask Me for something your size." Carver is said to have kicked at the ground, which drew his attention to a peanut plant. "Mr. Creator, show me the secrets of the peanut." He took the peanut back to his laboratory and went on to develop dozens of peanut-based inventions from peanut butter to axle grease. George Washington Carver changed the world.

"Just one idea!"

Just One Idea Can Change Your World

I looked intently at Jim. This wasn't what we were supposed to be meeting about. No matter—something big was happening right there in Jim's office. Jim wasn't much older than I—maybe five years or so. Yet he understood something about life that I hadn't yet grasped, and he wanted me to get the point.

And what is that point? Just one idea—that's all it takes in life to change the world. It's not complex.

That's what happened to Bill Gates, founder of Microsoft and the wealthiest person in the world. Back when most computers were the size of a tractor-trailer truck, Bill Gates saw the future—a computer on everyone's desk. But he wasn't alone—a few others had this same vision at about the same time. Most went about building computer hardware (monitors, CPUs, keyboards, etc.). Bill Gates stumbled onto something else: he created the software—the brains that ran the box—and let others deal with the hardware.

I remember my first encounter with "MS-DOS." In my first professional post-college job, I was used to Apple computers, so the IBM computers at my job seemed very clumsy. When the computer started up, it offered a blinking cursor, cueing the user to enter some alphanumeric commands, which seemed antiquated compared to the Apple interface. One of my coworkers told me that blinking cursor was MS-DOS. I wish I had taken the time to find out what the "MS" was in MS-DOS and invested in that little start-up company.

Interestingly, it didn't take long for MS-DOS to become an outdated operating system. Thanks to the initial work done by the research lab at Xerox, some guys at Apple began to adapt the concept "graphical user interface" (GUI) to the personal computer. GUI's what-you-see-is-what-you-get computer interface made the computer *usable* to the masses. Gates didn't invent GUI, but he was the best at adapting to the concept, creating the GUI "Windows" operating system that currently controls 97 percent of the operating-system market worldwide. Gates understood a simple concept: the computer was a platform upon which software would run, so build the brains instead of the box. It was one small idea that others missed, and now he's the wealthiest man in the world.

Sam Walton is another man with a powerful "one idea." He barnstormed across Arkansas, Oklahoma, and surrounding states to place his discount stores in small towns where big retailers dared not tread. He provided smaller towns with big-city discount prices and became the only game in town. When I moved to Oklahoma in the '80s, we had to venture outside the city of Tulsa to visit a Wal-Mart in the surrounding small towns. By focusing on small towns, Walton cornered a unique competitive advantage in the marketplace, building a breakthrough distribution network while continuing to cultivate his company's "small town" corporate culture. Only later did Wal-Mart move into the big cities, and by then Sam Walton had already captured the lion's share of the market. Today, Wal-Mart is not only the largest retailer in the world; it is the largest food retailer in the world, nearly four times the next largest.

This story, however, isn't about Bill Gates or Sam Walton and unimaginable wealth. It's about the Grassfire Effect and how you can expand your impact in your world. Right now. And it's about how a guy with a wife and kids, living in the heart of suburban America, took hold of a simple idea and changed a small corner of the world. Not the entire world. Just a small corner. And it all started with a simple conversation with a guy named Jim—a conversation whose message still burns brightly within me. That day in Jim's office, a big puzzle piece fell into place.

It's a message I hope will burn brightly in you as well. You can change the world—you just need a simple idea and a dream. The dream can take on many forms. The ideas are all around us. I'm sure you have a few ideas rattling around in your mind right now. All you need is one. And the good thing is, the idea doesn't have to be special or fancy or technical. Sam Walton put discount retailers in small towns. Wayne Huizenga, the owner of the Miami Dolphins, made his fortune picking up trash from businesses and hauling it out of town to cheaper landfills. Truett Cathy, founder of Chick-Fil-A, decided to put chicken on a bun and sell chicken sandwiches in the mall—long before anyone had heard of a food court.

Just one idea can change the world!

That's it. It sounds almost too simple, doesn't it—that "one ideas" are really the source of world-changing power? But it's true.

Tapping into Your Own Grassfire Effect

In the coming chapters, you'll read about one such idea that has ignited to reach millions of people, helping to turn the Internet from a passive instrument into an active tool that equips citizens to impact their culture. But that's only the backdrop.

This book really is about understanding how the world is changed one idea at a time, and how you can change your world. But the first step is this: you gotta believe. You have to be convinced that you can actually be a world changer. You have to take hold of the idea that your life can have a profound impact on those around you and that your "one ideas" can gain the momentum of the Grassfire Effect.

I left that meeting with Jim with a whole new outlook on life. I set my heart on seeking out those "one ideas" that could change my thinking and even extend my personal impact on this world. Nearly two decades later, I can see how taking hold of simple ideas has truly revolutionized my life, ultimately putting me in a position to discover for myself this secret of grassfire and apply it to my world. And just like Jim said, it all started with a simple idea. Or in this case, a small spark.

KEY EFFECTS

1. How is the world changed? One idea at a time.
2. You cannot escape your dreams. Every so often, something will happen to awaken your dreams in colors so bright it hurts your eyes.
3. You don't have to change the entire world, just your small corner—your world.
4. When setting out to change the world, start small. Don't despise seemingly small ideas that could have profound impact.

FIRE STARTERS

🔥 World-changing ideas often come in small packages. Can you think of three ways ideas have changed the world you live in? Think small, not big.

1.

2.

3.

🔥 It doesn't take a lot to be a world changer. One simple idea put to work can make all the difference in your world. Think of three ideas that have popped into your mind in the last few days. Don't judge the ideas. Just write them down.

Idea 1:

Idea 2:

Idea 3:

🔥 Do you believe that you can change the world? Or are you still convinced that someone else is destined to do great things? Take a minute right now to step toward launching your own Grassfire Effect. Seize this truth: you can change the world. Now make it official.

    I, _____, do agree and declare that I can change the world!

    Signed _____

KEY INSIGHTS AHEAD:

- *Where do sparks of ideas come from?*
- *How to foster more creative sparks*
- *What do I do once I get a spark of an idea?*

Chapter 2

That First Spark

Understanding the Source of Ideas

What will I tell my grandkids? I almost hate to admit it, but if I try to recall my earliest thoughts that led to Grassfire.org, that's the phrase that comes to mind: *What will I tell my grandkids?*

It was 1999, the final year of the millennium. What news highlights do you remember? Bill Clinton's impeachment trial. Monica Lewinsky's involvement. The plane crash of JFK Jr. And who can forget the infamous Y2K scare that was supposed to change the world as we knew it?

There was another story that dominated the news that year—the dot-com explosion. Hardly a day passed without another report of a twenty- or thirty-something, high-tech guru who had amassed a fortune simply by putting an electronic shingle out in the dot-com world. It didn't seem to matter if the company made money or even had a business plan. All that mattered was getting on the dot-com rocket and blasting to the top of the "new economy" stratosphere.

All of a sudden, people were making money—easy money, returns undreamed of a generation ago. And no matter what they did, these dot-com businesses seemed to prosper. Or, at least, they seemed to prosper on paper, with rising stock values unrelated to relative worth.

I remember reading a story that compared the founder of the newspaper in my city and his son. The founder had worked his entire life, building a large newspaper and diversifying into television and other industries on his way to becoming one of the richest men in the entire state of Virginia. Then the article told about this magnate's son, who had started a dot-com only two years before. In those two years of Internet entrepreneurial frenzy, his son had already amassed, on paper, more wealth than his father.

We all thought the Internet was going to take over our lives. Why would we need malls when we can go online and shop? The Internet would eliminate the middleman— no sales force or even buildings needed. And most of all, the Internet is really, really cool. Millions of people bought into that idea, throwing billions of dollars into developing the infrastructure that would radically redefine our lives.

There was a trickle-down effect to this stock market boom as millions of Americans jumped on board and saw their investments and retirement accounts soar. People talked about retiring in a matter of years, and the old rules of investing went out the window in favor of a never-ending rise in the stock market.

But as we all know, the boom went bust. Almost as quickly as the rocket took off, it crashed and burned— littering the landscape with dot-com DOAs and on-the-run CEOs who sold when stocks were high.

What really happened with the stock market was not much different from a Ponzi scheme in which early investors are paid out of funds from subsequent investors while the enterprise shows no real profit. The dot-com businesses were not making money; they were thriving off the rise in their stock prices. As long as stocks continued to sell at increasing prices, there was plenty of cash to keep the business afloat. So dot-coms continued to spend cash at phenomenal rates (remember all the dot-com Super Bowl ads?). But once the bubble burst, most of these companies disappeared in a Wall-Street minute. For those that survived, hundred-dollar stocks quickly became penny shares. Many of us still have some worthless stock certificates to show for it.

What My Future Grandkids Taught Me

But for a minute let's take a step back in time to those months before the bust—when excitement over the Internet was still revving up. I don't recall the exact day, but I know I was sitting at my desk, absorbing the daily bombardment of the Internet explosion, probably reading a story about some twenty-four-year-old cyber-savvy punk who started a dot-com between his college classes. Now he had a net worth in the hundreds of millions—and he still didn't comb his hair. Or tuck in his shirt. Or pull up his pants. But I wasn't bitter. OK, I was probably a *little* bitter.

I didn't have a bad life. In fact, I had a great life. I was married to the woman of my dreams, and that year Stacy and I celebrated our tenth anniversary. We had three beautiful little girls who all thought Daddy was the "bestest." We lived in a nice community of three-bedroom homes and friendly neighbors. I was running a business out of my home, serving as a writer for nonprofit organizations. But there was a great chasm between my financial picture and those brash, young Internet billionaires.

And that's when this thought went through my head. *What will I tell my grandkids?*

Somewhere way beyond all the money that was being made through the Internet, I knew deep inside of me that something revolutionary was happening in our world. The Internet *was* changing our society. Maybe it wasn't putting shopping malls and universities out of business, but it was creating a web of communications that eliminated distance even more than automobiles and airplanes had in the twentieth century.

The Internet *truly* made the world a global community. In the past decade, advances like Web sites, e-mail, chat rooms, instant messages, and online commerce have indeed changed the way we all live. In fact, as the Internet continues to extend its reach, the fastest growing segment of the online community includes senior adults. Our grandparents are getting into the Web!

I just knew that someday my own grandkids would come to me after sitting through an American history class or watching something on the holographic Super High-Digital History Channel about the Internet revolution and would ask me that question: "Grandpa, what were you doing when the Internet changed the world?"

Gulp. "Well, grandkids, I was very, very busy writing marketing materials." Hmm. That won't work. How about "I sat on the sidelines even though I knew the Internet was transforming society"? I guess I could just cut to the chase: "I missed it altogether."

At that moment, I had a rare glimpse of the future and my legacy. And I didn't like it. My heart sank. But at that same instant, something else happened—something quite unexpected. A spark was lit!

Where Sparks Come From

That's the interesting thing about sparks. You never quite know when or where they are going to light. The ingredients for a spark are really quite simple. In fact, you only need three things: fuel, oxygen, and heat!

Who can forget Tom Hanks in *Castaway* working for hours upon hours to get enough of a spark to ignite a fire. He found some dry grass blades and began rubbing two pieces of wood together. It worked for the Boy Scouts, so he rubbed and he rubbed until he thought he was going to go crazy . . . when it hit him — air! He needed to create room for the fire to breathe.

The nature of sparks is that they are unpredictable. When just the right combination of fuel, heat, and oxygen are in place, a spark will happen and a fire will ignite. In the western United States, grassfires can spark up at a moment's notice and burn thousands of acres. Interestingly, a spark from lightning ignites most forest fires. Millions upon millions of lightning bolts hit the ground every year and are occasionally ignited into flames. Sparks happen every day all around us.

That's the first important lesson of the "sparking" process: sparks of ideas — the initial concept that flashes through your mind at the genesis of the creative process — happen constantly. Consider the word *idea*. *The American Heritage Dictionary* defines *idea* as "something, such as a thought or conception, that potentially or actually exists in the mind as a product of mental activity." *Webster's 1828 Dictionary* draws on the etymology of the word to give an even clearer picture. *Idea* derives from the Greek word *idein*, "to see." The 1828 edition's definition of *idea* is "literally, that which is seen; hence, form, image, model of anything in the mind." An idea is something that happens in your head; something that is seen in your mind's eye.

The Brain and Brainstorms

But how does a new thought develop in your mind? The late Dr. Paul Brand described what happens in the brain in his book with Philip Yancey, *In His Image:*

Physiologically, the whole mental process comes down to these ten billion cells spitting irritating chemicals at each other across the synapses or gaps. The web of nerve cells defies description or depiction. One cubic millimeter, the size of a pin-point, contains one billion connections among cells; a mere gram of brain tissue may contain as many as four hundred billion synaptic junctions. As a result each cell can communicate with every other cell at lightning speed — as if a population far larger than earth's were linked together so that all inhabitants could talk at once. The brain's total number of connections rivals the stars and galaxies of the universe.[1]

Recent advances in technology have afforded neuro-scientists more insight. Dr. Richard Restak, in his book *The New Brain: How the Modern Age Is Rewiring Your Mind*, writes that new, noninvasive technologies are providing "windows through which neuroscientists . . . can view different aspects of brain functioning."[2] These windows are fascinating, but most agree that science is only beginning to scratch the synaptic surface of understanding what happens in the human brain.

The Explanatory Gap

Philosopher Joseph Levine coined the term *explanatory gap* to describe the inability of the material or physiological to explain the mental or psychological. An explanatory gap definitely exists in the field of neuro-science — knowing that billions of synaptic firings take place in the brain every moment of every day does not explain the mind of man. The "sum" of the mind will always be greater than the "parts" of the brain. For example, a renowned neurosurgeon who studied more than one thousand epileptic patients, using electronic stimuli to cause their brains to react, could not find the "mind"—the thinking, reasoning, creating, willing force of human life. The chemicals and the neurons of the brain simply did not explain the creative impulse of the mind.

Some are convinced that man will never crack the puzzle of cognition—what makes a person conscious, creative, and uniquely that person. Author John Horgan in *The Undiscovered Mind: How the Human Brain Defies Replication, Medication, and Explanation* summarizes his assessment: "I fear that neuroscience, psychology, psychiatry, and other fields addressing the mind might be bumping up against fundamental limits of science. Scientists may never completely succeed in healing, replicating, or explaining the human mind. Our minds may always remain, to some extent, undiscovered."[3]

Because of his use of the word *fear,* Horgan's conclusion appears to be disturbing to him and may be to many in the scientific community. That is because the dominant worldview of modern science is materialism. As a worldview, materialism does not refer to a desire to have things. A materialistic philosophy says that the material world—the physical world—is the sum total of all that was, all that is, and all that ever will be. Materialism says there must be a material or physical explanation to the questions of science.

But if you believe that the sum total of man is matter, then you are left with a huge chasm called an explanatory gap. What is the physical explanation for even one original thought popping into your head? Where do ideas come from?

A Metaphysical Answer

So the gray matter between your ears—the most sophisticated computer ever designed—is constantly sending off electric impulses through the tissue connections in your head to control your body functions, translate input from your senses, and enable you to communicate with the outside world. But if that were the entire process, you would be nothing more than a computer, gathering data, processing the data through a vast database of experience, and spitting out reports to the outside world.

There must be more taking place than just the physical brain connections. How else would you come up with any-thing original—the thoughts, impressions, and realizations that result in sparks of ideas? This is where it gets exciting because this is where humanity distances itself from every other living thing on the planet. This is where you become human. Original. Unique. With vast potential. *Unlimited* potential!

Up there in your head this incredibly fascinating thing happens. Sparks. Ideas. Original feelings that are uniquely you and not just the result of certain impulses. This process is happening thousands upon thousands of times each and every day. Neuroscientists tell us that the idea center of the brain is focused in what is called the nondominant parietal lobe. But that knowledge does not solve the riddle of you. Every moment of every day, you are piecing together your own ideas, impressions, thoughts, and feelings about the world around you. And no matter how hard anyone else may try, no one can quite figure you out and make you predictable. Psychologists spend their lives trying to do it. Spouses attempt in vain to do it. Parents try it with their teenagers. And bosses attempt it with employees. Yet no one can "get inside your head." It's just not possible.

That's because you are not an animal. You are a human. And there is a vast separation between you and the animal kingdom. Now, if you have accepted the theory (and it is a theory) of evolution, that last statement will challenge you. It might even offend you because in the evolutionary grid humans are simply another form of animal. According to this theory, the Homo sapien outcome is the result of natural selection, a random process of mutation and change. The only causal agent is the impersonal force of chance. But if everything is nothing more than random chance, then humankind is random chance and there is no moral force or purpose to being human. Life just spins to the next mutation. There is no hope. Life has no trajectory or momentum other than randomness.

If you believe in evolution, for the sake of trying to understand this thing I call the Grassfire Effect, try suspending your belief in randomness for just a moment. Imagine that someone somewhere caused everything around you. The trees. The birds. The oxygen you breathe. The clouds. The sun. The moon. Your favorite things. Everything.

Think about the ten thousand known species of birds, the twenty-five thousand known species of fish (with hundreds more being discovered each year), and the approximately one million known species of insects. Think about the vast array of colors that you see all around you every day. Ponder for a moment billions of galaxies each containing billions of stars. Then consider that the billions of synapses in your brain challenge the complexity of the galaxies.

Now stay with me. Consider that some personal force in the universe created all of this. It's not random. Every last bit of it was thought out and planned by Someone.

What would you conclude? I'm not looking for a theological answer, but a practical one related to the topic of our discussion.

How about this: Whoever created all this sure is *creative!*

It would take an incredibly creative mind to design the one million known species of insects, never mind the 350,000 known species of beetles alone! I emphasize *known* because some scientists now estimate that there could be as many as eight million beetle species in the world! That is some serious creativity going on.

Because this creative force is so creative, let's for argument's sake call this force Creator. (By the way, British scientist J. B. S. Haldane reportedly said that the incredible number of beetle species shows that the Creator must have "an inordinate fondness for beetles.")

OK, stay with me. This is so vitally important if you want to cultivate those sparks of ideas that will ultimately lead to world-changing grassfires. And we've almost closed the loop on this; there's only one more thing you need to get.

Your Creative Heritage

Now, what if this Creator who created all this stuff in the universe picked out one special item in the universe and fashioned that one item in a unique way—in the Creator's own likeness? (Again, I'm asking you to suspend your belief in evolution just for a moment. Stay with me.) So if that one item of creation was fashioned in the likeness (i.e., image) of the Creator, what would you expect to be one of the outstanding characteristics of that item?

The one bearing the likeness of the Creator would be creative! He would be brimming with ideas and concepts that are created seemingly out of thin air. He would translate that creative impulse into creative reality. He would be a firebox of creative sparks!

I would submit that this creative spark resident in you is one of the key characteristics that makes you human.

Creativity creates a great chasm between humans and the animal kingdom. Perhaps it could be argued that there is a creative spark in animals (I'm no expert in that field and will not try to debate it). But consider this: we tend to find animals most fascinating when we catch a glimpse of what seems to be personality or creativity or cognition or ingenuity in them. If we see dogs interacting as members of our families in our homes, dolphins playing in the surf, birds seeming to dance in the air, or cats turning their noses up at us and acting aloof even while they seem to be coaxing some affection out of us, we are fascinated.

We love to see personality and creativity in animals because we see a reflection of ourselves in the animal kingdom. We instinctively know that this creative spark is the highest form of life. When are you being most fully you? When those creative sparks are flashing through your mind, being gathered together in unique ideas created by you and then translated into your world through your actions. Why is this important to understand? Two reasons: first, creativity is who you are. It is inherent in your makeup because you are human and were fashioned in the likeness of the Creator. Sure, that's my opinion. But there are only two opinions on this; the other is that you are the result of mere randomness and are nothing more than a combination of chemicals that require an explanatory gap to account for why you are who you are.

Second, creativity and the sparks of ideas remain mysterious domains. The source of ideas lies somewhere beyond the mere physical realm—the gray matter of your brain alone does not explain the total process. At the end of the day, we are merely *creative*, while He is the *Creator*. Thus, the realm of ideas is not something we can own or control. But we can tap into it.

Not a Material World

A few decades ago, Madonna sang about being a "material girl in a material world." That song is somewhat dated now, and so is the philosophy that went along with it. The fact is, this is not a "material" world. Materialism is the philosophical result of evolution—assuming the chance, physical world is all that there is. But as I have noted, materialism alone does not account for the human mind—the thinking, reasoning, and creative process that happens somewhere between the material connections in our heads and hearts. The brain is one of the greatest pieces of evidence against evolution and materialism there is.

That means the creative process is ultimately a process of . . . faith. By faith, I mean a realm that lies somewhere beyond pure reason in which every cause and effect is clearly understood. Creativity resides in the realm of faith—ideas actually *do* pop into your head. No amount of reasoning can explain the ultimate source of ideas, and creative people know this full well. Those first sparks of ideas that give birth to creative breakthroughs come out of the realm of faith. And that is a place you must dwell to cultivate world-changing "one ideas."

Tapping into Your Creative Reservoir

While we cannot control the creation of sparks, certain environments or activities will foster more creative sparks in you. Such scenarios are different for each person. Some people do their best work in the morning, while some like the late nights. Some like total solitude to get the creative juices flowing, while others find their best ideas in a crowd.

Just a few years ago, neuroscience believed that the brain's capacity for growth and change—its plasticity—leveled off some time around adolescence. Now, science is learning that the brain is in a constant state of flux and growth that continues into adulthood. That means your capacity for creativity has not necessarily reached its maximum if you have passed your formative years. Your brain power can grow and change. You can train yourself to increase your creative capacity and cause more sparks of ideas to fire inside your head.

So what environment or activities get your creative juices flowing? What about the creativity of those around you? What can you do to encourage your spouse's creative gifts? How about your kids' gifts? Your friends'? Coworkers'? Employees'? These are vitally important questions if you want to generate the sparks that lead to grassfires. In the Grassfire leadership team, we often get so consumed with daily operations that we can easily lose our creative edge. We recently discovered that we must step away from the daily tasks once a month as a leadership team to pause and reflect and recharge our creative batteries. That monthly strategy meeting is the most important event on our calendar because it reignites our sparks.

One of the ways I tap into the creative reservoir is through songwriting. I write tons of songs. It's like creative calisthenics for me. And virtually every song comes together in a somewhat mysterious way. I get an idea for the song, a few chords on the guitar, a few words, or all of the above all at once. Some songs are written in minutes. Some sit on the shelf half baked for months. Most of them never leave the circle of my family and my close friends. But each new song reminds me afresh of the mysterious and invigorating sparking process.

The sparks that give birth to ideas are bouncing around inside every human mind virtually all the time. Think back to how you thought when you were a kid. I have five young children and am continually amazed at how quickly they can bounce around from one flight of fancy to another. They create imaginary worlds with dolls and toys and trucks while sitting in the middle of the living room. They bounce back and forth between their imagination and reality without even blinking. Maybe that's because their minds are freer to be creative; they are willing to express externally the sparks of imagination and creativity that are stirring in their minds.

Remember that sparks need fuel, heat, and oxygen to thrive. Now think back over the past few days. Can you recount two or three creative sparks that flashed through your mind? If not, then you probably aren't giving those sparks enough "oxygen" to even register in your brain. You may be putting out the sparks before they have time to be recorded in your memory.

If that's the case, this book will help you fan the creative fires in your mind and turn them into wildfires of creative energy that compel you to take action.

The Spark of Grassfire

Back in 1999, somewhere in my heart and mind, a spark was ignited. I can't say it was of the purest motives (fear of having nothing to say to my grandkids!), but that's just fine. Perfectly pure motives are very hard to come by, and the search for such perfection in motivation can easily lead to the "paralysis of analysis." If we spend too much time analyzing our own motives, the spark will die out before the flame is even lit.

I began to look at the world around me differently. Instead of regretting that I was being left behind by the Internet revolution, I began asking a simple question: What can *I* bring to the Internet? What skills, knowledge, abilities, resources, or experiences did I have that could apply to what was happening on the Internet?

That's when the idea of Grassfire was born.

Remember, each person is a uniquely created and image-bearing individual. I'll never see the world through your eyes, and vice-versa. Each of us finding his or her place in the world is really a process of learning to apply that which is uniquely "us" to the world around us. The funny thing is, we often think of our uniqueness as a liability. Maybe we have been told over and over again of our faults, so that we only see the negative. Or we despise our own gifts because we feel they are too basic or common to be considered gifts. "Oh, it's nothing to be a mechanic/teacher/homemaker. Anyone can do it." I know people who are good with numbers but think nothing of it. A friend of mine looks in amazement at me because I can write, but he is a world-class photographer. It's an easy temptation for me to think nothing of writing and for him to think nothing of photography. But maybe my particular uniqueness makes writing one of my gifts and photography one of my friend's gifts. What a concept!

Apply *You* to Your Idea

So in 1999 I set out to apply *me* to the Internet. What did I know? I was an experienced development writer for nonprofit organizations. I could write in a way that communicated an organization's vision and motivated people to take part in that organization.

But there was more. Thanks to one key mentor, I began to understand what is at the very heart of every business, every nonprofit organization, every church, and every community.

My mentor, Bill, opened my eyes to this point while talking with me about a large, well-known nonprofit organization. This organization had an annual budget in excess of $100 million and a majestic campus that included a world-class university, state-of-the-art television broadcasting facilities, and a daily television show that aired across the nation and in dozens of countries. This organization also owned one of the area's premier hotels among other holdings.

Bill asked me a very interesting question about that organization: "Steve, what do you think is this organization's most valuable asset?" Almost immediately I suggested the buildings, the university, maybe the cable television network. With each guess, Bill smiled and shook his head. I was stumped.

That's when Bill told me what makes that nonprofit (and every organization) really tick. "It's not the buildings, the school, the television studio, or hotel," he said. "It's the supporters. They made everything you see happen, and without them, the organization would quickly wither away."

Bill said that the organization's supporters were its most vital component because they provided the funding and backing that made everything happen. It's much the same with every organization and business. Where would Gap or Lands' End be without its supporters (customers)? Where would a church be without members?

What really matters is the *network* that the organization creates and inspires. Everything else is window dressing.

Something else helped me spark the Grassfire idea: I love issues and the culture. At my core, I want to think through the issues with the grid of my Christian faith and have an impact on my culture. Just five years earlier in 1994, I had finished a master's degree in public policy, thinking it would prepare me for a career in politics. So I immediately embarked on my career in . . . direct-mail fund-raising! During this time, my love of issues stayed with me. I can remember many intense debates with my coworkers Jim, Linda, Lawrence, Johnny, Tom, Rich, and others in our department. Current events was part of our daily diet. We lived and breathed the "hot" issues of the day, and the process was preparing me for the spark to come.

Move ahead to 1999. I'm thinking about how the dot-com people have missed something. They missed the very heartbeat of the Internet—what Bill had taught me about the core of every organization. I know I'm on to something. I'm still writing direct-mail letters, but the spark is getting oxygen. *If only I could apply my desire to interact with culture and impact current events to what I know about the core of every organization.*

Suddenly, a spark! That's it! Grassfire!

The next chapter will cover precisely what this spark I call "Grassfire" is. But before we move on, grasp how the sparks of your ideas can take hold. Remember that you were created to have a constant flow of creative sparks—creativity is a vital component of who you are. Creative sparks are happening all the time; often the best ones come in the most unlikely times and places (like when I was regretting what my grandkids would think of me). But that's just the start. The next vital step is to sort that spark through your own perspective—your "grid" of your unique qualities, abilities, and experiences. Don't be afraid of who you are. Don't underestimate your unique qualities, desires, abilities, and experiences. View your spark of an idea through your passions (what drives you and thrills you to your core), and before you know it, your own personal grassfire will be lit.

KEY EFFECTS

1. You were *created* to be *creative* and have sparks of ideas; it's who you are.
2. Materialistic evolution falls short in explaining the creative mind.
3. Creativity happens in the realm of faith; ideas literally "pop" into our heads.

ᶗ4. Discover the environments or activities that foster more creative sparks in you.

ᶗ5. Once you have a spark of an idea, the next vital step is to run the spark through your own grid; apply yourself to your world.

FIRE STARTERS

🔥 Take hold of this truth about your creative nature by personalizing the first key concept above:

I, _____, was *created* to be *creative* and have sparks of ideas. This is my birthright.

🔥 Certain environments will foster more creativity in you. For me, songwriting is a breeding ground for creative thinking. Perhaps for you it is reading, biking, debating, walking, getting up early, or staying up late. List six activities or environments that encourage creative thinking in you:

1.

2.

3.

4.

5.

6.

🔥 List ten characteristics about yourself below. These characteristics can be personality traits, professional experiences, or perspectives on life—anything that helps make up your personal "grid." Once you have listed ten characteristics, think about that spark of an idea in the context of your grid.

1.

2.

3.

4.

5.

6.

7.
8.
9.
10.

Chapter Notes

1. Paul Brand and Philip Yancey, *In His Image* (Michigan: Zondervan, 1984), 127.
2. Richard Restak, *The New Brain* (Rodale, 2003), 3.
3. John Horgan, *The Undiscovered Mind* (New York: Simon and Schuster, 1999), 10.

KEY INSIGHTS AHEAD:

- *What is the main thing in life?*
- *How to fan sparks of ideas into flames*
- *Learning from the new Internet model*
- *Why do most sparks die before they become grassfires?*
- *What does respect have to do with grassfires?*

Chapter 3

How Grassfires Are Ignited

What Is Life Really All About?

Back the '90s, the Internet was a "field of dreams." The catchphrase from the similarly titled Kevin Costner movie described the mind-set of most of the dot-com business ventures: "If you build a Web site, people will come."

It seemed to be working. Dot-com stock prices soared and daily Wall Street reports indicated that the "new economy" of the Internet had left the "old economy" (of actually building and doing things) in the dust. It seemed that all you had to do was open your electronic shop in the World Wide Web and people from all over the planet would be knocking at your door.

It's difficult to even remember now, but only a few short years ago, most of us had never even heard of the Internet and e-mail. I recall clearly my first encounter with the Web. A friend of mine named David, just back from college, wanted to show me something over lunch. So he pulled out a laptop right there in the Olive Garden

restaurant and began trying to explain to me this phenomenon called the Internet. He showed me what a "Web
page" was and a report that tracked "hits" (visits) to a
Web site he had built, which showed thousands upon
thousands of hits from all over the world.

I immediately went back to my boss, John, and told
him about what I had seen. John had been in direct marketing for two decades. The key to his success was his
dogged commitment to tried-and-true principles mixed
with a willingness to try new techniques. John set in
motion a process for our $100-million-plus nonprofit to be
among the first to venture into Internet marketing.

Long story short, we did it. Despite much opposition
from other departments, we actually launched a Web site.
I can remember John looking at me and saying he felt that
in some small way we were making history. We were blaz-
ing a trail.

Just like that line from the baseball movie, we built it
and people came. But due to that organization's internal
struggles, that site ultimately failed. Still, I knew we were
onto something.

Skip ahead to 1999. The dot-com mania is at its peak
and my spark has been lit. I knew I had to try something —
anything — on the Internet. Plus, I kept thinking about
telling my grandkids that I didn't take advantage of the
Internet. That would be like my grandparents telling me
that they resisted those newfangled contraptions called
automobiles.

The Old Internet Model

With these thoughts in my head, I began looking at the
Internet from my vantage point. I knew there had to be
more to it than building a Web site in this field of virtual
dreams. Still, my first thought was to stick to the movie's

and the Internet start-up mantra and build a Steve Elliott Web site that advertised my writing services. Clients and prospective clients could come to the site and find out about my offerings. That's what every Internet entrepreneur was thinking and doing. There used to be reports of millions of Web pages being added to the Internet every day. But one small flaw occurred to me: Why would I or someone else go to these sites more than once? Let's face it: how interesting is it that I can write letters? It just didn't seem very compelling even to me. So I considered the next line of thinking in old Internet strategy: build a "destination" Web site, hoping that if enough content is on the site, people would come back repeatedly. That model still works for some (the Drudge Report to name one), but I simply didn't have the resources to do such a thing. After all, even in those early Internet days the *New York Times* was spending more than $100 million annually on its Web site! How could I possibly compete?

I call this line of thinking the "old Internet model"—the if-you-build-it field of dreams. But as we all soon discovered, it was difficult to push enough "traffic" to a Web site to sustain a business model. Do you remember something called NBCi? It was NBC's attempt to build a destination Web site. NBC aggressively pushed the concept of NBCi, hoping that it would become one of the gateways to the Internet. They ran countless ads and developed tie-in features between NBCi and their regular network programming. The concept limped along for months and probably cost NBC hundreds of millions—all in a futile attempt to drive traffic to their site. Where's NBCi today? That's my point. The old Internet model simply wasn't feasible and was a prime cause of the stock market collapse. The Internet field of dreams died.

What the Internet and Life Are About

The breakthrough for me came in 1999 when I began filtering my desire to do something on the Internet through my own grid. What was my own grid telling me?

E-mail!

The most important and useful aspect of the entire Internet was e-mail. E-mail was more powerful than Web sites because e-mail connected me to people—real people, people that I knew. As my friend and pastor Oscar often says, "The church is not the building; it's the people." Take away the people and you don't have anything. The same is true of the Internet. I'm not talking about zillions of impersonal hits. I'm talking about living, breathing Internet users who maintain their lifeline of personal contacts using e-mail. The heart of the Internet will always be people, and e-mail is the strongest connection to the widest cross section of real people.

Consider what succeeds on the Internet and you'll find a people-focused theme. Look at eBay. The idea is so wonderfully simple—it's a user-friendly forum that directly connects sellers with bidding buyers. In essence, it's a giant flea market. How about Google? It's a search engine that seems to be unlike any other because it actually connects the user to the right links and the right information, usually in one or two searches. EHarmony.com is a Web-based matchmaking service that uses its patented technology to help singles find the right partner. The common thread is clear: the best things on the Internet connect people to people.

But this people-to-people principle is not just true on the Internet. As my mentor Bill said, every organization, business, and group is totally dependent on and constantly looking for one thing: people.

The network is everything. Life is really about people. And that very element is the core of what we call grassfire.

The guy who drove this point home to me most of all

was my dear friend Mike. Mike is the smartest, most creative guy I know. Mike can do anything he wants. In college, Mike was the guy who worked two or three jobs and actually had a car. He always had money and was constantly busy. Yet there was something else about Mike— his whole orientation in life centered around people. Over the past twenty-one years, I've watched Mike time and again pour his life into core friends. Money was simply a tool in his hands—he continues to give little or no thought to accumulating it for himself. Mike was my best man, and he's repeated that role about a dozen times (I think he belongs in the *Guinness Book of World Wedding Records*). Think about that: one guy pours his life into enough other guys to be a *best man* over and over again!

I mention Mike for two reasons. First, I'm pretty sure Grassfire would never have happened without him. His friendship shaped the way I think. He turned me from a task-oriented individual into a people-focused person. So when it came time to think about the Internet, I was not distracted by technology or Web sites or anything else—I was thinking about people.

Second, I hope my mention of Mike brings someone to your mind. I hope you have a Mike, a friend who sticks closer than a brother. A friend who can hear you share about your spark of an idea and then give you advice, criticism, encouragement, or a reality check—whatever is needed to get that fire going. Mike became one of my first sounding boards for this spark of an idea.

As I mentioned, I have a master's in public policy, and my daily orientation is toward current events. I knew I wanted to use the Internet to impact the way society thinks about the important issues of our day. I began to ponder: Why not use e-mail to build networks of people who want to take action on issues that are vital to their lives?

And just like that, Grassfire was born.

I conceptualized the process. I'd e-mail all my friends and ask them to take a stand with me on a hot issue. The e-mail would direct them to a Web site where they could register their support. The system would send them an e-mail they could forward to their friends and help rally others. The end result would be networks of citizens built to take action on key issues. Those networks could then influence our leaders and demand action.

I know it sounds so simple, but at that time, I had never seen the strategy we now call "viral e-marketing" applied to issue-driven petition campaigns. One of the key people I shared the idea with was a good friend named Kurt. He and I had many lunches, talking about this network-based Internet model that flew in the face of the old Internet model that was still getting all the rave reviews. We joked that this would be the first Internet-based organization *without a home page!* Who cared about home pages, anyway? E-mail and personal networks were where the real energy of the Internet was. (Interestingly, we didn't have a home page for Grassfire until nearly a year after its beginning. We were so convinced that our new network-based model was the way to go that we intentionally forsook the old home-page model.)

Keeping Important Things Important

The network-based model works because life is very much about people. Why, then, do we tend to forget the prime importance of people? The same reason many of the great sparks of ideas that come into our minds never ignite a fire. The fact is, it's very difficult to keep important things prioritized in daily life. That's because life is really, really busy. Have you noticed? It's so busy that we run and run and then we're so tired that we sit down and "veg" in front of the TV. Then it's time to go to bed. We wake up late and run and run to lunch. After lunch, we run right to dinner, fighting traffic and all the other people who make our lives even busier. After dinner, we're too tired to do anything else so we watch TV. You get the picture.

It's hard to be mindful of the people around us. And it's nearly impossible to find time to, as they say in football, "take the ball down the field" on the world-changing ideas that are sparking in our minds. We need help in a very practical way.

Enter Robert. Robert is a friend of mine who is a small-business consultant. Around Christmas 1999, I hired Robert to do a business review of my direct-mail writing business. We met. He reviewed all my materials. We met some more. It was one of the best things I've ever done as a businessman (of course, I followed it up by neglecting to hire Robert again the following year).

Robert told me many things, but two stuck with me. The first one came while we were having lunch at a restaurant. He just looked at me and said, "I see you in a more executive leadership role in your industry. Not this coming year but soon." Robert could see something in me that I couldn't see myself. At the time I was a one-man shop— my business was me. To do better, I had to write faster or work more hours. Robert saw something else.

Secondly, Robert treated me and my business with respect, as if what I was doing was a *real* business. He didn't see just one-man-shop Steve. He saw a young entrepreneur operating a real, live business. He gave me as much respect as he might give a Fortune 500 company. Robert said that I needed to act like a real business. To do that, I simply had to have some research and development goals. I was pretty tired at the time. It was the end of a long year of sole proprietorship. Federal taxes were about to take another pound of flesh from me. I really did not want to do much of anything.

"Do I have to?" I asked.

Robert smiled and slowly looked up at me. After a pause, he said, "Only if you want to be a *real* business, Steve." (Emphasis in the original.)

Ouch.

I looked at Robert. He looked back at me, half laughing now — not because he knew he was right but because he knew the message was getting through.

I briefly pondered what Robert had just said, looking away to take in the environment. It was one of those moments in life that would forever be frozen in my mind. What Robert had said was extremely important. There was a huge difference between sitting in a Business 101 class and reading about goals and living out that same lesson while sitting in that restaurant.

I looked at Robert and said, "You know, I do have this *one idea* that I've been developing in my head for some time now. It involves the Internet, and I think it fits really well with my business."

Robert didn't even ask me what the idea was. He just said, "Then make it a goal this year to test it."

How Goals Get You There

So I set a goal — a specific, measurable goal. It was only a few words and went like this: *Test using Internet for petition drive to create database by end of third quarter.*

That was my spark, run through my grid, and set out as a goal to be achieved over the coming nine months. Only fourteen words. A goal.

Once that spark has formulated into an idea, the next vital step is to set a goal — the stage that trips up a lot of would-be world changers. They get a spark. They even run it through their own grid. They talk to a few friends about it. Their core friends say, "Go for it." But nothing happens. Why? Because they never set a meaningful goal.

Countless books have been written on how to set goals, so I'll sidestep that discussion except for this one point: make sure the goal is specific, measurable, and time-sensitive. It is more important to set a goal than to strive for a perfect goal. Set a goal and get started. You can always modify your goal later.

But why are goals so important? For perspective, let's consider why we do not set goals. While there are lots of goal-killing excuses, the barrier I face most often is a low opinion of my own ideas and ultimately of myself. I get these sparks and then I dismiss them just as quickly because of those clouds of doubt. This book is a great example. I have come up with many, many reasons not to finish *The Grassfire Effect* even though this book is about helping anyone take their spark of an idea and turn it into a world-changing force. Doubt is always there to discourage me. Fortunately, the publisher set a goal (otherwise known as a deadline).

Perhaps the same is true for you. Maybe while reading these pages you have had a spark ignite or reignite in your mind and heart. That vivid, Technicolor dream you once had is coming alive again. All the ingredients for a grassfire are there, ready to set off across the field of your life! But there is something else lurking nearby—those doubts fueled by a low opinion of yourself or your idea. Unless you take action quickly, those doubts will be a wet blanket on those first sparks of your grassfire.

At this crucial point, when the sparks have been ignited, it is vitally important for you to show some respect for those sparks. And you can do that by setting a goal. Goals force you to treat your ideas (and ultimately yourself) with respect. A goal is an endorsement, recognizing that the spark of an idea is valuable and worth your time and attention.

Perhaps the spark for you is to become an architect. When you look at your world and run it through your grid, you discover that you get excited about how buildings are designed. Maybe your parents or your friends noticed that you were always designing structures in your head and on napkins at restaurants. After a little research, you find out that architecture is for you. Now it's time to show some respect for that spark. Set a goal: *Graduate in four years with a bachelor's degree in architecture.* Can you see how that goal brings respect and dignity to *you* and to the spark?

As Robert said, *real* businesses have goals. People who understand their intrinsic worth as human beings created in God's image have the courage to set goals. I say courage because in addition to respect, goals breed another powerful force: accountability. I was recently talking with some of my partners at Grassfire about where we want to go in the coming months, and we began to set some goals. We realized that we were doing very well, but we lacked direction and focus. We lacked goals. So we set out some goals. That's when I realized that by setting out the goals, we were determining our future. Not in a precise way, but certainly in a directional sense. One of my associates said matter-of-factly, "If we set these goals, we're going to reach them."

That's because goals breed accountability—to the goal itself and to other people involved in achieving the goal. Quite often the only motivating factor in moving forward is the goal itself and the accountability it demands. For example, about four times a week I jog a few miles. Most mornings, I do not want to run. My body aches a bit and my mind can think of many other things to do. But I have a goal: to achieve a certain level of fitness and maintain a certain weight. So I lace up my running shoes and head out.

The Heart of Grassfire

During the nine months that followed my conversation with Robert, the idea spark that was born in my head and fostered and nurtured by people continued to develop. I worked with my goal in sight: *Test using Internet for petition drive to create database by end of third quarter.*

I decided I wanted to build a stronger bond between the people who would participate in this e-mail-based petition drive. What if we could let petitioners know how many people responded to their e-mail and signed the petition? What if we could then let them know about the subsequent "e-generation" that got e-mails from those friends? We could tell the initial petitioner that twenty or even fifty people signed the petition because they took a few minutes to get something started.

That's the very heart of Grassfire. Our slogan is "Real Impact. Real Feedback. Real Results." Everything we do is centered on helping people build these networks and expanding their own impact. Instead of *one* vote, a Grassfire member can have an exponential impact that extends to ten, one hundred, one thousand, or even ten thousand or more! (I'll share more about this in coming chapters.)

My friends served as a sounding board for getting from that simple goal to an actual test by the end of the third quarter. Somewhere in that process, I recommended a name: Grassfire. It just fit so perfectly. The Internet is the fresh breeze that spreads the spark to others through e-mail. If this actually worked, it would be just like a grassfire.

The imagery was perfect. But when we checked, the domain name address was already taken. For a moment, my heart sank. How could I ever be a dot-com without a dot-com address? The echo of my grandchildren began to haunt me once again.

But wait: dot-net was available. And doesn't dot-net fit better, anyway? Grassfire isn't about "commerce" in the old Internet model. It's about networks! Networks of concerned citizens eager to see their impact grow through the Internet. So it became Grassfire.net. Over time, we were able to secure .com and .org and now Grassfire.org is one of the leaders in online citizen activism.

The next chapter deals with what happened when, to our surprise, the fire of Grassfire actually started to spread. But before we move on, consider the lessons I'm learning from Grassfire and apply them to your own spark. After the spark of your creative idea is lit and you start running that spark through your own grid, you'll never make it to the next step unless you have two vital ingredients: *friends and goals.*

Without friends and goals, your creative spark will most likely be prematurely extinguished and your grassfire will never even be seen. Remember, life is about *people*. My spark of an idea—Grassfire—is all about networks of people. Your personal grassfire will also be about people. Take a moment right now and think through how your grassfire spark is really about people. How does your idea serve people? Begin reflecting on and refining your people-focused grassfire spark.

In addition to your idea being about people, it will be fanned into flame by people. I've mentioned some key people in my grassfire: my mentor Bill, my friend Mike, Robert the business planner, and Kurt, my friend and sounding board. There were others as well, like Jim and Ron, two guys who heard about Grassfire long before there was any reality to it during lunch breaks. My wife, Stacy, has always been my strongest believer. She celebrates every new creative spark, even the ones that never kindle into a roaring fire.

So begin identifying the handful of people in your life with whom you can trust this spark and ask them to be a sounding board for you. This principle applies in virtually any setting at any time in life. Maybe you feel like you are "just" an employee in some dead-end job. You have some ideas that could change your job and change your company, but they are going nowhere. Find a friend, take him to lunch, and instead of complaining about your boss, tell your friend about your spark that could revolutionize your company. Then ask your friend to meet with you once a month and talk about this spark until a plan develops or it becomes clear that the spark isn't going to light.

I have found that meals are the best forum for sparking ideas. The dynamic that happens around the table is unlike any other setting. If that spark of an idea dies out, I'm sure by then another spark will have lit somewhere inside of you. Trust me, your friend will find time for lunch once a month . . . especially if you treat.

Secondly, at some point in the sparking process you have to set a goal. I am convinced that if Robert had not challenged me to act like a *real* business and set research and development goals, Grassfire would never have happened. So once your spark starts developing in your mind and among your close personal network, it's essential to set an attainable goal. As the Good Book says, "Write down this vision; clearly inscribe it on tablets so one may easily read it" (Hab. 2:2). There is something about putting things in writing that changes our perspective.

But what if you don't achieve your goal?

Who cares! As we tell our kids, the most important thing is that we give it our best effort, that we really try to achieve that goal. There was a Michael Jordan commercial in which he describes all the times he missed the basket. His career totals show more than twelve thousand missed field goals (and another two thousand misses in the playoffs). The greatest basketball player of all time failed to make the varsity team his sophomore year in high school. But few would ever consider Mike a loser.

Consider baseball, in which a batter can succeed just three out of ten times in getting a base hit and still wind up in the Hall of Fame. Reggie Jackson holds the career record for strikeouts (2,597), and he is in the Hall of Fame. Nolan Ryan lost 292 games (the second most all-time) and is in the Hall of Fame. The New York Yankees, my favorite team, have lost more World Series (twelve) than any other team has won (nine).

Failure is relative and a necessary part of success. No, you may not perfectly achieve what you set out to do. Even if Grassfire had never happened, I would have learned something in the process that would have led to something else. Grassfire would have become part of the prologue to some other story. In fact, Grassfire is certainly a chapter in the bigger story that is my life. So set a goal and go for it!

Perhaps this book would be more compelling if my name were Bill Gates and I could back up my ideas with my fortune. But I'll never be Bill Gates. And that's OK. That's not my dream. I didn't have his one idea. And neither did you. And perhaps it's better that my story of Grassfire isn't so overwhelmingly large that you think your idea is insignificant. In the scope of the world, Grassfire is very small. But in *my* world, it's a big deal. Your idea is just as big. And when you run your spark through your grid, add in some close friends, and set a real goal, soon the fire will start to spread.

KEY EFFECTS

1. Life is about people. Your life should be about people.
2. Your grassfire idea must be about what life is about (people).
3. Find key people to help fan your spark into flame.
4. Grassfires die out quickly without goals.
5. Goals add two vital ingredients to your grassfire: respect (for yourself and your idea) and accountability.

FIRE STARTERS

🔥 Because life is about people, your grassfire idea must be about people as well. Write a few sentences about how your grassfire spark impacts people.

_____

_____

_____

_____

🔥 List three key people in your life with whom you can share your idea. Find time in the next three days to contact them.

1.

2.

3.

🔥 Are you ready to turn your spark into a practical goal? Try writing out your goal in just one sentence. Is your goal specific, measurable, and time-sensitive? Don't try to get a perfect goal; just show some respect for your grassfire idea by putting down a _starter_ goal on paper.

My _starter_ goal:

KEY INSIGHTS AHEAD:

- *Do you know your birthright?*
- *The risk of reality*
- *How do you refine your dream?*
- *Bringing your dream to reality, step-by-step*
- *The importance of timing and getting started!*

Chapter 4

From Spark to Flame

Turning Dreams into Reality

How about 'Amerigo'?"

My wife knew I was joking. We'd been playing the name game for our fifth child, and I admit I may have been scraping the bottom of the barrel. From Maximillian, Placido, and Shadrach, to Herschel and Dingbang, I'd run the gamut with the same result. Stacy would roll her big, brown eyes, and I'd return to the baby-naming book.

This time I found myself thumbing through the As. What about Ahab, Aimery, Alfonso . . . Amerigo? Wait a minute. Amerigo. I know that name. Amerigo Vespucci.

OK. I didn't name my son Amerigo. Still, I was intrigued because I remember enough of American history to know that our continent (and our country) got its name from this guy, Amerigo Vespucci.

Understanding Your Birthright

Names are very important. Your name is a part of who you are—you and your name are inseparable. Each human being answers to a particular combination of phonograms strung together into much more than just a word; it's a name. Even though other people undoubtedly share that name, it's still yours. How many times have I been in a public place and automatically turned my head upon hearing "Steve"? I can't help it. I'm Steve. Those sounds are like a homing beacon for my soul. I must respond.

And behind your name is some particular meaning. Perhaps it comes from the etymology of the word or perhaps your name is a family name, connecting you to generations past. Your name may simply reflect your parents' selection, and that's enough. After all, your name is your parents' first gift to you. They did not give you life—that's a gift beyond the realm of any human. But your parents did give you a name.

Stacy and I had already had this privilege on four occasions and were working on number five. My daughters each know what their names mean because we recite the meaning to them and even pray this meaning over them. It often serves as our bedtime blessing: Anna Marie (fragrance of His grace), Hope Elizabeth (our hope is in the promises of God), Kirsten Joy (joyful follower of Christ), and Lauren Elise (consecrated for Christ's victory). As they grow, we can already see how the meaning of their names is reflected in their character and ultimately in their calling.

Back to Amerigo, the guy for whom America is named. He was a contemporary of Christopher Columbus, but the two continents these explorers discovered are not called "North Columbia" and "South Columbia." They're called North America and South America. That's because a

German cartographer named Martin Waldseemuller had read about Vespucci's journeys to the New World and, in 1507, he labeled an area of what is now northern Brazil "America." Waldseemuller literally put America on the map and unwittingly gave a gift to hundreds of millions of people.

What does this have to do with what I am calling the Grassfire Effect—this exciting process whereby your ideas can become sparks that can light a fire to change your world? Well, it just so happens that *Amerigo* means "industrious."

Try to write a history of America without a major theme being our industrious nature. "Characterized by earnest, steady effort; hard-working." That's what industrious means, according to a 1969 edition of *Webster's*. An argument could be made that America is the most industrious nation in the history of the world. If you have ever seen a replica of the *Mayflower* or another boat from those first settlers, then you know what kind of intestinal fortitude it took to come to America in the 1600s. The first settlers were legendary in their industrious nature and their willingness to sacrifice—first for survival and then to build a prosperous future for generations to come. In the 1700s, the grandchildren of those first settlers took on the task of forming "a more perfect union" founded upon certain "unalienable rights." Their industriousness created the foundation for the longest-lasting democratic republic in human history. By the 1800s Americans were taming the West, building great cities, connecting this great landmass by railroad, and cultivating new crops. The 1900s were rightly called the American Century as this land carved out a preeminent place in our world, all the while taking in the outcasts of other lands.

Why did so many immigrants come to America? To have a chance at what the world calls the American dream.

I am a product of the American dream. My mother is a first-generation American, and my father is the son of immigrants. What is the American dream? It's an opportunity to turn your dream into reality. That's what this chapter is about. And it may be the most important concept for you to grasp to take advantage of the Grassfire Effect. This is where nice-sounding ideas get refined and put into practice It is this idea-to-reality stage that has, in my opinion, separated America from the rest of the world.

Hopefully, the preceding pages have helped you understand the vital importance of discovering those "one ideas" that can change your world. Perhaps you have a better understanding of the process by which sparks of ideas are birthed and how those sparks are refined when you run them through your own grid, get feedback from close friends, and finally articulate those ideas into real goals. Without those first steps, you'll never experience the grassfire.

But quite frankly, articulating your goal can be the easy part because there is likely a great chasm in your mind separating your dream from reality. That's where I found myself as soon as I mustered up the courage to write my dream of Grassfire into a real goal. Remember the goal? *Test using Internet for petition drive to create database by end of third quarter.*

The First Step May Surprise You

The day after I wrote the goal, I did something very, very important. It was something that would ultimately determine the success or failure of not only this effort but my entire life, marriage, career . . . everything.

So what did I do? I did nothing.

That next day, I made no progress toward my goal. Nada. Zip. Zilch. Was I burned out from sparking the dream? Did I need to take a rest after taxing my brain so heavily? Not even close. I was excited and full of adrenaline. I couldn't wait to get started. Except for this thing called timing.

One of the most common mistakes people make after defining a goal is getting ahead of themselves; pressing too hard, too fast, too much, too soon. Imagine a baby who has just taken his first steps and now is so filled with excitement he can't wait to go chasing after his brother and sister. What happens? Fall down, go boom. Even the baby realizes that he must take his time or suffer the consequences. By rushing too fast, you, too, could suffer consequences that lead you to abandon your goal before it gets a chance to change your life.

Once I set my goal, I still had a business to run, a wife to love, kids to raise, the yard to rake (or at least to *think* about raking). Rather than being consumed by my goal, I controlled my excitement and did what I'd been doing for years: I lived my life.

I don't believe we have to come crashing out of the gate like a thoroughbred with our goal. Instead, remember the baby—take incremental steps toward your goal. Trust yourself. Trust your idea. Trust your goal (I gave myself nine months because I had a feeling it would take some time to put the pieces together).

Speaking of puzzles, this pausing step in the process is like when you first dump the pieces onto the table. There's no sense being frantic about immediately assembling what's in front of you. Good jigsaw strategists just do the basics—they find the borders and the corners. They group similarly colored pieces together. They make order out of chaos and are content to take small steps toward a bigger goal. So that's the first key step—keep doing your stuff and you'll find the corner pieces.

The Refining Process

While you are doing your stuff, something else is happening that is essential. Whether you know it or not, your mind is carefully refining this idea that became a goal that will soon be a reality. That's why I say don't be in too much of a rush because the clearer the picture you have in your mind, the better your chance of actually getting your idea tested.

As discussed in the last chapter, while my idea stewed in my head, the name Grassfire came about. Every day, I continued to rehearse the idea in my mind and to others. Each time I told the story, my own idea became more and more focused in my mind. I could imagine sending out that first Grassfire e-mail to my fifty friends. I could see them getting excited and joining in the process and forwarding it to their friends. Although I knew very little about computers, I thought through precisely what would be needed to track the impact of each person, so that we could tell idea initiators that their influence was spreading like a grassfire. Grassfire happened in the reality of my mind long before we sent the first e-mails out.

You see, it's not enough to taste your idea. You must chew on it for awhile. But even that isn't enough. Next you need to swallow your idea and get it inside you. But the process doesn't end there. As my dear friend Ron often says, you must "pass it through your intestines" until the idea becomes part of you. In digestive terms, that is what is happening during this vitally important do-nothing phase. Your idea is becoming part of you.

The entire model for Grassfire.org came together during this process after the goal was set and before the idea became reality. Months have turned into years, and we are still operating off that same core model—with refinements, of course.

There comes a day when the idea must become *reality*. You must *build* it. Making it a reality is different from thinking about what works in theory, which reminds me of a saying in our Grassfire team: "That works in Theory." There's just one problem: none of us live in a town called Theory. We live in a crazy, unpredictable, risky place called Reality. Theory is nice and comfortable; Reality is zany and uncomfortable.

Seven Steps to Turn Your Dream into Reality

So here it is. The moment you've been waiting for. *Steve's going to tell me how to get from here to there. He's going to give me seven things to do to build my dream.*

Actually, I'm not . . . because I can't. Even if I gave you my seven steps, they probably wouldn't work for you. You may be tempted to follow them, and that could be disastrous for your dream. Remember, you are a unique creation. You are *you* and no one else.

In reality, getting to a goal is simple. You point your face in that general direction and you take a very bold baby step or two. Though you start slowly, taking small steps, each one brings more knowledge and more decisions. And each step will take you closer to your goal.

At some point in these steps, you will have to ask yourself some tough questions. Namely, can you take your dream to reality without the help of anyone else? Can you do this yourself? If you answer yes to that question, then please go back to the beginning of this book and start over. Either you didn't dream big enough or you have missed the central point of the Grassfire Effect: people are at the core of every business, every organization, every church, everything. Every idea, no matter how obscure, gets better when you bring together a team of people to build it. It might be one other key person. It could be your spouse. It could be some of the same people who helped you think through the concept, but not necessarily so since you sought those initial people for their *wisdom*—you needed wisdom to filter your idea. Now you are looking for *knowledge* and *expertise* to make your dream come alive.

Finding Experts in Reality

In my case, having looked at all the necessary ingredients to make this prototype of Grassfire, I knew what I needed: a computer expert. I'm a pretty good computer *user*, but that's about it. I can surf the 'Net but don't really understand how the 'Net works. I knew this couldn't go very far without an expert or two, but I had to go fairly far to get one: from my home in Virginia to a small town in rural Iowa, in fact.

It happened while I was on the phone with my brother-in-law Sam, who lives outside Des Moines. I was still in my do-nothing phase, cogitating the idea with my circle of friends. During our conversation I once again rehearsed the concept with Sam, explaining how Grassfire would work. He asked lots of good questions. The best of all was, who's going to build it? He saw immediately that the missing ingredient was an information technology (IT) team to actually execute the idea.

I told him that I didn't know yet, but I was looking. Then I did the next logical thing. I redirected the question at Sam: "Do you know anyone whom you trust that could pull this off?" I asked.

Sam rephrased my question: "You mean, 'Do I know someone who can do this who won't steal it from you?'"

Well, that was exactly what I meant. This is a very risky step in the dream-to-reality process because it's very easy to lose control of a really good idea once other people are involved. But get ready because you will likely have to get other people involved.

The Leap of Trust

A personal reference is still probably the best way to connect with the right people. That's why I strongly recommend starting with your personal network. And be sure to ask for referrals from people you enjoy collaborating with. More likely than not, if you get along with someone, you'll get along with someone they get along with!

When Sam said he had an IT contractor whom he trusted, I knew that person would work well for me. That's when Sam recommended Bob Pritchard. The most important decision I made in this process was to trust my idea to Bob. Bob remains the key person in the Grassfire team — he's the hub around which our entire IT team operates. Without Bob, this either would never have happened or someone else may have co-opted the idea. But it almost didn't happen with him.

I picked up the phone and called Bob. No answer. So I left a message. A few days later, I left another message. And another. No response. You see, Bob was really busy doing his own business. He didn't know me from Adam. And because he's a computer guy, friends often approach him with their latest and greatest ideas. He blew me off.

I was about to give up but decided to call one last time. I knew I'd get an answering machine, so I placed the call from my cell phone while driving about seventy miles per hour down the highway, rushing to another meeting. I wasn't holding back this time. I wanted to have urgency in my voice. I strongly emphasized my need to talk right away and again mentioned the connection — Sam.

Bob got the message and finally decided to call me back. Perhaps he knew he'd hear from Sam if he didn't call or maybe he heard something in my voice. Perhaps he heard that spark on his answering machine. Whatever the

reason, Bob and I finally connected. I told him the vision
I had for Grassfire—the vision I had carefully honed by
telling it again and again over the past months. As it turns
out, this was the most important telling of my story. Bob
was the right guy, and I needed him to catch the vision, to
see the spark. He did and the fire spread from Virginia to
Iowa.

Now consider how important my do-nothing phase
was. I talked to Bob about six months after I first made the
goal. During those six months, I had been bouncing this
idea of Grassfire around in my mind, doing whatever
research I could. Mostly, I was telling and retelling the
story. By the time I talked to Bob, I had my story down
pat, and I was fairly convincing that this Grassfire idea
might work.

Over the next days, Bob, his brother Randy, and I
went back and forth with this idea until Bob had caught
my vision and made it his own. Within a short time, we
both began asking the next obvious question: When? It
was late July 2000 when I first talked to Bob. If I had told
him "next spring," Grassfire would never have come to
fruition. But I had set a time constraint in my goal. And
the goal demanded that I respect the idea.

So I boldly said "September" because that would meet
my "end of third quarter" goal. We had about six weeks. Bob
knew it was time to get to work. He began writing the code
that would make the idea reality, while I continued to work
on my end, which brings me to another very important component about the dream-to-reality phase.

Your Personal Risk

In addition to the risk you take in involving other
people, you are also going to have to risk some of yourself.
I cannot tell you what your exact risk will be—it could be
your time or your savings account—but turning the dream

into reality requires that resources start flowing. One more thing: you can budget all you want, but do not expect your budget to hold up to reality. That's because as you move your dream into the reality phase, it will morph and take on a life of its own.

Then more questions will occur to you. I wondered how Grassfire would actually get launched. What should the e-mails say? How about the Web site pages? And most important, what issue would we tackle first?

Each question was a subset of the goal that I set out months before. Each answer was another baby step that brought us closer to realizing the goal. The answers led to more questions, which demanded more resources to find the answers. And so on.

Before we knew it, September had arrived and we were ready to launch. This idea called Grassfire—the small spark that began with my shallow concern about what my grand-kids would think of me for missing the Internet revolution—was about to become reality. I can remember the excitement. Would it actually work? Or had all my thoughts and bold pronouncements about this idea been way off? Could I really come up with an idea that would actually work? What if it failed?

In the next chapter, I'll share what happened when those flames started burning beyond our control. But before we move on, reflect on steps that help you turn your dreams into reality. Remember, don't get ahead of your-self—timing is everything. So start taking some baby steps, including your do-nothing phase of thinking and research-ing and telling and retelling your story. Those steps will cause you to ask more questions, which will lead to more steps. And search for those key trustworthy people who, like Bob, can help you actually turn your dream into reality. Then get ready to add more resources—your *human* resources—to turn your dream into reality.

You Can Do It!

Above all else, remember that you *can*, in fact, turn your dreams into reality. I believe it is the birthright of every human being—what the founders referred to when they said every person is "endowed by their Creator" with the "unalienable right" of the "pursuit of happiness." This birthright, although available to all, continues to separate Americans from the rest of the world. If you are an American, then that German cartographer unknowingly gave you a gift: you carry in your name this great "industrious" heritage. All around you are stories of the American dream realized. This birthright comes from many factors (such as our nation's profound heritage of faith, free-market ideals, religious and personal liberty, and property rights), but regardless of the source, it's in the air! It's yours to claim!

Back in the 1980s, many experts were predicting that the Japanese would soon surpass the United States as the world's preeminent economic power. We heard reports of astronomical land values in Tokyo. We were told that most of the world's largest banks were Japanese. Special reports showed us that Japanese companies were buying up California. But behind the scenes, something else was happening. Steve Jobs. Bill Gates. Michael Dell. The high-tech revolution. Silicon Valley. The Grassfire Effect was already well underway, and breakthrough dreams were becoming reality. By the '90s, America was back at the center of it all, and I haven't heard much of Japanese economic domination lately.

Now all the talk is about China—China this and China that. Everything's made in China. More cell phones and TVs are in China than America. But I'm still putting my chips on that place where dreams become reality. That industrious land where earnest, steady effort actually bears fruit and where ideas can start grassfires that change the world.

And it all starts with *you*. Each generation of Americans ("industrious ones") must produce millions of American dreams to keep this nation the envy of the world. And that means you must take hold of your name — your heritage, your birthright—and commit to turning your dreams into reality.

Finally, remember the importance of timing. In our family we have a saying, "There's always a Middletown Road" —a reference to my grandmother's long search for retirement housing in New York City. The months dragged on into years as my grandma waited for just the right housing opportunity to come up. It seemed to take forever. Then at just the right time, an apartment opened up in a new retirement community on Middletown Road in the Bronx in a very nice community. Now whenever my aunt and I are discussing some big branch on the decision tree of life, she always reminds me that timing is everything: "There's always a Middletown Road coming soon." Some dreams take many years to become reality. But that's OK when you have the confidence of your birthright.

By the way, we did come up with a name for our son: Samuel Michael. "One who is heard of God and understands God's world." I think that's a great gift for our son.

KEY EFFECTS

1. The industrious American dream is your birthright; go for it!
2. Move steadily from dream to reality but don't get ahead of yourself.
3. There are no seven easy dream-to-reality steps. Every person and every process is unique.
4. You will have to risk to move from dream to reality.
5. You should count the cost of moving from dream to reality but don't hold yourself to the projections.

FIRE STARTERS

🔥 What timing have you set for your dream-to-reality phase? _____. Is your timing realistic or unrealistic? Too long? Too short?

🔥 Let's count the cost and do an inventory of what you will have to risk to move from dream to reality. Take three minutes to estimate the personal investment you will have to make to get your idea to the test phase.

Number of hours: _____

Hard cost in dollars: $_____

Will you have to forsake other earning opportunities? If so, estimate that amount here: $_____

Number of evenings you'll have to work and miss out on your family/friends: _____

Number of sleepless nights: _____

Number of favors you'll have to call on: _____

🔥 Multiply the above answers by five and place those answers below.

Number of hours: _____

Hard cost in dollars: $_____

Will you have to forsake other earning opportunities? If so, estimate that amount here: $_____

Number of evenings you'll have to work and miss out on your family/friends: _____

Number of sleepless nights: _____

Number of favors you'll have to call on: _____

🔥 Are you still willing to pay the price? What if it is double that?

___yes___no___maybe

Chapter 5

When the Fire Spreads

How Success Will Challenge You

There's a TV commercial that mirrors how we felt the day we launched Grassfire.org on the Internet. In it, a handful of people are gathered around a computer monitor, beginning to celebrate the launch of their e-commerce site. Finally, after all the preparation, they can take orders!

The employees watch as the computer monitor flashes "Number of Orders." Next to that field is the number zero. They eagerly await that first online transaction. Then, it happens! The first order comes in and the "0" flips to "1." A roar is heard among the team—an immediate release of all the tension from weeks and months of hard work and planning.

Then the 1 flips to a 2, then a 3, and quickly to a 4 and a 5. They can't contain their excitement—it's actually working! They look around and cheer each other. But then they look back to the monitor and see the counter scroll faster and faster. It shows 20 . . . 30 . . . 50. Now every employee is staring at the screen in utter disbelief. Then 100 . . . 200 . . . 500 . . . 1,000 and so on.

The room is silent. Despite all the planning, all the preparation, all the hours of work, the team simply isn't prepared for one thing.

Success.

Your Greatest Challenge

This may come as a surprise, but the greatest challenge in life is not failure; it is success.

Why is success difficult? Because success comes with strings attached—strings that extend to your very heart and soul. Our small Grassfire team was about to experience success as depicted in that television ad, and how we handled that success would determine just how long this creative spark would stay lit.

Thus far, we've seen how world-changing ideas begin with "sparks" of creativity. We've discussed how to take those creative sparks and run them through our own grid—apply the spark to our way of thinking, our experience, our perspective. We've seen how setting specific goals and building a team to achieve those goals can bring us from dream to reality—from idea to actual prototype. But what if that spark actually succeeds?

Interestingly, even though each spark of an idea starts with a dream of success, the success phase is the most difficult. That's because very few people actually plan to succeed, picturing in their minds what success is. We've all dreamed of the trappings of success—the big car, the bigger house, fabulous vacations, and everything that goes with it—but those are just the trappings. I'm talking about what success *feels* like and how its handled once you achieve it. I know that sounds different from what you may have heard, but in a very real way, you cannot entirely prepare for success. At some level, you must simply live through it.

A Picture of Success

As our launch date of September 15, 2000, approached, we spent some time trying to define success. The goal was to *test using Internet for petition drive to create database by end of third quarter.*

But what would be success? How would we know if this idea actually worked? Because we were starting this effort by letting our friends and family (maybe two hundred or so people) know about it, I thought that if we saw one thousand or (dare I imagine?) ten thousand people take part, that would be success. I didn't want to be disappointed, and so I told myself that as long as we saw growth we would have something that could become an effective tool for grassroots citizen involvement.

At this same time, I began to see that the cultural battle of our day was focused on one group of Americans: the Boy Scouts. That summer, the U.S. Supreme Court had issued a very controversial ruling in a case from New Jersey (*Dale v. Boy Scouts*). This ruling involved a local Scout leader (James Dale) who admitted that he was homosexual. He wanted to retain his leadership position in the organization, but Scout officials removed him from his post. He filed suit, and the case was appealed all the way to the U.S. Supreme Court.

Grassfire's First Issue

Dale v. Boy Scouts was argued intensely and watched closely. The central question of the case was, could a private organization set its own standards for leadership? The Scouts felt they had to have this right. Scouting is based on a mentoring system whereby men teach, train, and show by their lives the path for young boys to become

men. Scouting has been a vital part of American society
for decades and has contributed greatly to raising up boys
to pillars in society.

Let's take a moment for a metaphor. Living in south-
eastern Virginia, I've gotten used to tourists infiltrating
our pristine beaches. Few are aware of the hidden dangers that lurk just beneath our breaking waves—not
sharks; it's even more dangerous. In fact, despite the
warnings, a number of swimmers and surfers are lost each
season to riptide. These unseen underwater currents can
pull even the strongest swimmers out to sea. And for
those who are unaware of the dangers, exhaustion and
drowning can easily result.

With the Scouts, there's a similar unseen agenda in our
nation that is pulling tens of thousands of unsuspecting citizens into an abyss, and the worst part is that most don't
even realize it's happening.

This agenda centers on destroying what we call the
"traditional family" and the God-given roles of men and
women in society. Some saw this case as an excellent
opportunity to break down these traditional roles. These
groups assumed that if they could force the Scouts to
accept a homosexual in a leadership position, it would
force private organizations of every type to accept alterna-
tive lifestyles—thus further undermining the morality and
core values our nation was founded upon.

To the surprise of many, the U.S. Supreme Court
issued its ruling siding with the Scouts. The justices said
the Scouts have a constitutional right to set their own leadership standards and bar homosexuals from positions of
leadership.

Case settled, right? After all, if we learned anything
from twentieth-century politics it is that the U.S. Supreme
Court has the final say. The Supreme Court has, in
essence, the final law*making* authority in our land

(although this was never the role the founders intended). The Supreme Court would regularly interpret laws and then not only rule on the law but also write lengthy "opinions" which were, in essence, new legislation.

But not everything was settled. Instead of heeding the advice of the U.S. Supreme Court, a backlash ensued against the Scouts. Every few days, we learned of another United Way agency or local community that was instituting its own counter-ban against the Scouts. Any group that discriminated against other groups (i.e., homosexuals) would be denied funding and other services.

The Scouts were on the run. And those who supported the Scouts were worried about being labeled homophobic. The backlash gained momentum throughout the summer and into early fall. That's when I decided to test the grassfire concept on a petition drive that supported the Scouts. What if we could rally thousands of people to take a stand for the Scouts? What if we could show the nation that people all across this country believe in the values the Scouts uphold and stand against this wave of homosexual support?

I had a personal stake in the issue. As a boy, I was involved in Scouts, and as an adult I could see how the Scouts helped to reinforce key values. In fact, now more than ever, Scouts represent the very arrowhead in the cultural debate shooting through our land.

Luck and Success

The values the Scouts represent are at the center of all we do at Grassfire. But we almost didn't pick the Scouts issue to launch Grassfire. At that time, we were considering several different issues, but I wanted to find the most potent topic possible to test the Grassfire concept, and Scouting became that issue for a broad and diverse group of citizens.

Were we lucky to have picked the Scouts? Perhaps, in that I acknowledge that there are factors in my life beyond my control that impact me greatly. But luck is not some impersonal force. One of my favorite thinkers, George Gilder, says that what most people call luck is simply the providence of God. Luck happens. Providence happens. It's how we respond to those providential happenings that determines how lucky we really are.

As our launch day approached, we seemed to get lucky. Through an unusual set of circumstances, we were faced with an open door of opportunity to have our petition mentioned on one of the largest national radio programs. We debated. Are we ready? Will the system work? Will it hold up?

Remember, I am in Virginia. Bob and the computers are in Iowa. I'm not a computer guy, so I asked Bob, "Are we ready?" Bob briefly thought about it, then said, "Let's go for it!"

So we made the calls and the contacts. And we waited to see what would happen.

It didn't happen. We didn't get mentioned on air. We were slightly discouraged, for everything had seemed so right. But we went back to work and back to our scheduled September 15 launch. Bob met the target date and we launched.

Then we noticed the system wasn't working. Technical glitch. No one can sign up on the petition! Fortunately, we had not done our full launch yet. We could easily recover from this and relaunch in a few days.

Then it hit me. What if we had gotten on that national radio show? What if thousands of people had tried to access this Grassfire site, only to get error messages? Sure, the damage would not have been irrevocable, but it certainly would have made lighting our first grassfire much more difficult. Time and again in the life of Grassfire, our team has seen this providence. Time and again, we would try to do something that we thought was really smart, only to be foiled in our attempts. Later, we would breathe a sigh of relief that we had been protected from what we had tried to do.

Failure and Success

What does this have to do with success? First of all, success comes in many packages. Sometimes what we think is failure is really success because it takes us to where we need to go to achieve a new level of success.

Rumor has it that successful people fail the most. Maybe they understand that failure is success from a different vantage point. As noted above, failure can protect you from your best intentions and can point you in a new direction.

Shortly after graduating college, I landed a job in my area of study, accounting, with one of the world's largest accounting firms. Almost immediately, I failed. At best, I was a mediocre accountant. I technically didn't get fired, but I just couldn't work up any enthusiasm, so I left that job. In fact, I left accounting altogether. (Somehow, I don't think the accounting world has ever regretted letting me go!) Were my years of college study in accounting a complete waste of time and money? Not at all. Although I couldn't see it at the time, my failure in accounting freed me to move on to other things.

Not long after, I took a job in marketing and communications. It suited me perfectly. I could write and communicate a company's vision. I was overjoyed . . . until I got fired. So within twenty-four months of graduating college, I had left my chosen profession and been fired from my second real job. Unemployed, recently married, broke, and depressed, I thought things could not get much worse.

Sure, I wallowed in self-pity for a season. But what I didn't realize was something else was happening beneath the surface—something far more important. These failures I experienced were guiding me in another direction. Without those failures, I might still be in a job I hated, making a lot of money, wondering what I used to dream about. Instead, these failures set me on the course to my dreams—and I didn't even know it. Again, it was one of the most difficult seasons in my life. I felt like a failure. But a good friend of mine helped provide perspective. He told me that a time would come when I would rack my brains to remember this trial of unemployment. He was confident that this season would point me in a direction that I needed to be pursuing.

Success is in many ways incremental steps of failure. That's not a pessimistic view of things; I still believe the glass is half full. But the fact is, until you can handle failure, it's all but impossible to recognize success when it hits you.

My World-Changing Day

The initial failed launch of Grassfire had worked to our advantage. Two days later, on September 17, 2000, Bob said he was ready and we could go ahead with the launch. For most people in the world, it was just another day—get up, go to work, eat lunch, work some more, come home, eat dinner, watch television, go to bed. But for me, September 17 was a world-changing day. That one small spark of an idea was about to change *my* world.

That's precisely what success does: it changes your world. September 17 marked a turning point in my professional life and in my perspective. We sent out a few e-mails alerting our friends about the backlash against the Scouts. And then it happened just like we thought: other people—from all across the globe—were doing just what we asked them. They were signing the petition, taking a stand for the Scouts, and using e-mail to alert their friends.

Our Grassfire Effect Begins

And just like in that TV commercial, Bob and I watched the "counter" spin. Soon we crossed one thousand signers and couldn't believe it. A fivefold increase! I'll never forget the first time we reached one thousand signers in a single day. I was in Fort Lauderdale when my cell phone rang. It was my wife, Stacy, who was watching the counters, telling me what the numbers were. I turned to my buddies, Mike and Doug. One thousand people *that day* had spread the grassfire for the Scouts! We were amazed.

In only a few weeks, we saw ten thousand, then fifty thousand, and then one hundred thousand people take a stand for the Scouts. It was unimaginable. One hundred thousand people—all from a simple spark of an idea. It truly was a grassfire. We had an idea about what we thought would happen, but success was breeding a new phenomenon: the Grassfire Effect.

Remember the process? What had started out as a small spark of an idea had been fanned into flame by running it through my grid, setting goals, working with people, and investing time and resources. Now that flame was spreading across the field of involvement at an exponential rate. So we tasted success, but did our success impact the Scouts?

Real Impact for the Scouts

By late October of 2000—just a few weeks after our Grassfire launch—thousands of citizens were joining us every day to take a stand for the Scouts. At the same time, more and more reports were surfacing of United Way agencies and government authorities taking action *against* the Scouts.

All this time, we had been tracking a story in New England in which the Connecticut Commission on Human

Rights was getting ready to issue a ruling that would deny the Scouts access to public facilities in that state. With the date of the ruling fast approaching, our tiny Grassfire team sprang into action.

We prepared a special message to our Scouts supporters, letting them know about the Commission's pending vote. We listed some key contact phone and fax numbers and an e-mail address in the update. Even we were not prepared for what happened next.

Thousands of citizens responded to the Commission with phone calls, faxes, and e-mails. The volume of e-mail shut down their in-house mail server. Their switchboard was lit up nonstop for days. All because citizens were mobilized for action, ready to defend the Scouts no matter where the attack might originate.

Legislative Victory for the Scouts

Since our launch, events like these have become commonplace for Grassfire. Citizens wanting to make an impact unite over a cause and make a difference. As with the Scouts, citizens were eager and motivated to make a difference, and that's exactly what was about to happen.

The following year, we continued to track the Scouts issue and saw an opportunity for a major victory in a bill called the Scouts Equal Access Act. This bill would deny federal funding to any local public school that discriminated against the Scouts. If a local school district banned the Scouts from using its facilities, then that district would forfeit federal dollars.

A senator from North Carolina was the first to introduce the Scouts Equal Access Act, and we tracked its progress through the Senate. As the vote approached, we rallied citizens to send tens of thousands of Western Union Mailgrams to Senate leaders and to call and fax their legislators.

Something else happened. Our staff began calling leaders in the House who had previously expressed support for the Scouts to ask them if they were going to place a companion bill up for a vote in the House. Call after call, it seemed as if no one on the House side even was aware of the Senate amendment in support of the Scouts.

Then one of the contacts we made on the Hill called us back—just one day after our call. Representative Van Hilleary was going to introduce a House companion bill to the Scouts Equal Access Act. By now our team of Grassfire Scouts supporters had grown to more than a quarter million, and we alerted our team of the pending votes in the House and Senate. Over the next few weeks, and after thousands of personal contacts from our Scouts supporters, both bills passed—the Senate bill by a narrow 51 to 49 margin.

But the battle for the Scouts Equal Access Act was not over. In fact, opponents of the bill were ready to ambush our side and make matters worse for the Scouts. Senator Barbara Boxer had offered in the Senate a competing amendment to the Equal Access amendment. The Boxer Amendment would make it illegal for schools to discriminate against any group based on their views of sexual orientation. This would mean the Scouts' views against homosexuals in leadership positions couldn't be discriminated against, but neither could a school refuse access to a homosexual, lesbian, bisexual, or transgender group.

As is the case with most bills, the Scouts Equal Access Act was sent to House-Senate committee. In Congress, the House and the Senate operate as separate legislative bodies. While both houses may be voting on similar bills, unless the wording is identical, the bills must go to a conference committee where the differences are reconciled. There was just one problem: the conference committee that was reviewing the Scouts Equal Access Act was stacked *against* the Scouts.

This is where our e-network really made a dramatic difference. Remember, to most people following this issue, we had already won. The bill passed both the House and the Senate. The major media followed the story and reported the "victory" for the Scouts. But behind closed doors on Capitol Hill, that victory was about to be taken away. So our team rallied additional Scout supporters. One of our staff members then carried more than three hundred thousand pro-Scouts petitions to our nation's capital for a major rally followed by a delivery to Senator Ted Kennedy's office—one of the members of the conference committee. In addition, we arranged for another mass delivery of hand-delivered Western Union Mailgram messages to the key swing voters on the conference committee. In all, more than twenty thousand Mailgrams were delivered.

A few weeks later, the conference committee voted and passed the Scouts Equal Access Act. It was the culmination of months of effort by our Grassfire team of Scout supporters, and leaders on the Hill took note.

Did we make the difference? In politics, it is difficult to truly take credit for any legislative victory, but I can say this: our Scouts team lit up the switchboards on this issue and our calls to the House helped encourage leaders there to take action. And the feedback we received from Hill leaders on both sides of this issue indicated that Grassfire supporters truly made a difference.

For example, one of our team members e-mailed us about when he called his senator (who opposed the Scouts Equal Access Act), noting that the staffer who answered the phone said, "You're with those Grassfire people, right?" That Senate office had received enough calls to know the source of the activism. On another issue, we helped send so many faxes to Senate leaders that we actually received a fax back from one office saying, "Please stop . . . Burned out fax!"

After the final vote supporting the Scouts in the conference committee, Representative Van Hilleary—who led the fight for the Scouts in the House—invited our team to come back to Washington, D.C., for a photo op. Representative Hilleary's team told us that the final push of phone calls and Mailgrams to the committee helped make the crucial difference between victory and a behind-closed-doors defeat.

This is only one example of how the success of Grassfire has translated into a real impact on our nation. When we started, we viewed success rather narrowly—building the networks of citizens. Now our understanding of success extends to the *real impact* our Grassfire networks are having and can have on our nation. We define success as equipping citizens with the tools they need to have an impact and then bringing together more citizens to have a greater combined impact.

When Success Gets Personal

Yes, my life changed on September 17. But I didn't realize it right then because I wasn't manning the operations center. Bob, on the other hand, experienced the life-changing force of success almost immediately. I have often pictured Scotty from Star Trek in the engine rooms, running from console to console, uttering those unforgettable lines, "I'm givin' 'er all she's got, Captain!" Bob had become my Scotty. Grassfire quickly consumed his life. He stopped answering his computer consulting calls. The Grassfire engine room was calling instead.

I don't think Bob slept much for the next two months. This *thing* happened—success. And somewhere around September 18, Bob had to make a decision that would determine whether this enterprise would even get off the ground.

Would he let the success get personal?

You see, had Grassfire failed that day, Bob would have sent me my final invoice and gone on with his life. He has a great life. He lives in Maxwell, Iowa, a small town we often call "Mayberry without the traffic." Bob and his brother Randy had a successful computer consulting business. They made a good living. They don't have to lock their doors. And their buddy next door brings them roast beef sandwiches from his general store for lunch like clockwork and just puts it on their tab.

But Grassfire actually worked, and that success would demand nothing less than a big chunk of Bob.

Bob took the plunge. I think Grassfire just connected with his personal "grid" so perfectly that there really was no choice. He's a grassroots guy—a down-to-earth American who holds tightly to the core values of faith and family. He loves politics and saw in Grassfire an opportunity to put together all those pieces: computers, Internet, grassroots, politics, impact on issues. With no promise of any financial return, with no knowledge of how this whole Grassfire thing was going to work out, Bob dove in headfirst. He's definitely a cliff diver in entrepreneurial terms.

My plunge came a few months later when Bob and Randy called and told me that there were no more resources left. For the first time, they laid out just how much time, money, and effort they had expended to get us to this point. After working day and night to keep the Grassfire engine room running—and literally abandoning their paying computer consulting work—the well had run dry.

It was my moment of decision. They could keep the engine room going, but I needed to find a way to make the funding work immediately. And we needed to turn Grassfire from an exciting idea that actually worked into a real organization that could support this phenomenal growth. Or we needed to simply abandon the idea and go back to our lives before Grassfire.

I knew what was at stake. Yes, I had invested my money and my time with no return. Yes, I had blazed the trail to take this idea from spark to reality. But now, the cost of success truly caught up with me. Grassfire needed a big chunk of *me*.

It was November 30. I hung up the phone and sought Stacy. We sat down and talked through what this meant, trying to count the cost. I asked Stacy for her advice, knowing my decision would greatly affect her life. And it was a huge risk.

She looked back at me with those same eyes that saw something in me when I was an unemployed twenty-four-year-old with no money, a pile of debts, and no real career path. She had stood by me while I got back on track and put me through graduate school. She had encouraged me to leave a salaried job for the world of self-employment. In fact, she had always extended to me her eyes of faith even when all I could see was doubt. This was no different.

"What do you want to do, Steve?" she asked.

I knew she was going to stand with me no matter what the future held. "If I don't do this, I'll always regret what could have been," I said.

"Then let's go for it," she said.

Together, we embarked on one of the most tiring, trying, and rewarding seasons in our lives.

Can You Recognize and Handle Success?

Success sounds wonderful, but we often don't recognize it because it can arrive as incremental steps of failure. If you don't recognize your future success in each failure, you'll get derailed. Take comfort in the fact that failure is often a stepping-stone to success. And when the opportunity for success comes, remember that future success will likely be linked to incremental failure. In other words, calculate the cost for success in your life and be ready to pay.

One final note on success: it has an interesting way of putting a megaphone to your failures. Those little mistakes you used to make that no one else noticed now seriously impact other people—friends, coworkers, business associates. Some of these relationships may never be restored. That has been the single most painful lesson that success has taught me. It's the highest price I have paid.

In section 2, I will lay out for you precisely how the Grassfire Effect causes your spark of ideas to change your world. It's the fundamental principle of growth for any individual, business, or organization. But before we move on, ask yourself this:

Will you recognize success when it comes? And can you handle it?

To help you answer those questions, first take a mental account of your recent failures. Record them at the end of this chapter. Then draw a line down the middle of the page and write down the success that came out of (or could come out of) each failure. Remember, successful people aren't afraid to fail because the road to success is paved with failure.

Second, get ready for success by always staying one step ahead of your own comfort zone. Challenge yourself every day, even in the little things. Do something different to break your routine. Run around the block. Turn off the TV. Go to work a half hour early. Skip a meal one day. Read a good book. Pray. Build something.

Success will change your life, and more important, it will change you. But it simply cannot happen unless you prepare yourself. That might mean throwing away some old habits and cleaning out some dark corners in your life. It may take some time and some of the cleaning might even be a little painful. But it's necessary—and it's worth it. Remember, success isn't cheap. It has a price. And the price is *you*.

KEY EFFECTS

1. The greatest challenge you will face in life is not failure but success.
2. It is essential to develop a picture in your mind's eye of what success looks like.
3. Luck seems to happen along the path of success; understand what luck really is and respond accordingly.
4. The road to success is paved with incremental steps of failure. See your failure through the eyes of success.
5. Success will surprise you, test you, challenge you, and change you.

FIRE STARTERS

In the left column below, list some recent failures in your life. In the right column, write down a success that did occur or could occur from that failure.

Failure   Successful Outcome

How can the idea that is sparking in your mind right now become a success? In a few sentences, record what your picture of that success is.

_____

_____

_____

_____

_____

_____

🔥 To prepare for success, you need to stay one step ahead of your comfort zone because success will stretch you. List five simple things you can do to challenge yourself today by changing your routine or trying something new.

1.

2.

3.

4.

5.

Section 2
Inside the Grassfire Effect

KEY INSIGHTS AHEAD:

- *The Grassfire Effect defined*
- *The Grassfire Effect as a life principle*
- *How the Grassfire Effect causes businesses to grow*
- *The impact of a negative Grassfire Effect*

Chapter 6

Grassfire Effect Defined

A Principle for Growing Your Life

Annette had no idea how far her personal grassfire had spread. All she knew was that her heart had been stirred by the unspeakable events of September 11, 2001.

The wife of a retired naval commander, she had watched in horror as hate-filled terrorists struck the Twin Towers and the Pentagon. She saw how our nation responded with three simple words: "God Bless America." She knew in her heart that this was the answer; this was what our nation needed.

"I see this song not only as a song, but as a prayer to God for His blessing upon our nation," she said. "The United States of America has been blessed by God to be free to pursue life, liberty, and happiness. And this song is a cry from the heart for God's blessings on our nation."

Our Grassfire team had been watching America's response to 9/11 and, like Annette, we saw hope in those three words.

Just hours after the New York City skyline changed forever, and with the Pentagon still ablaze and another hijacked plane in smoldering ruins in Pennsylvania, members of the House and Senate stood shoulder-to-shoulder on the steps of the Capitol and sang what composer Irving Berlin called his "most important song."

Hearing our leaders spontaneously sing—mostly off-key yet unashamedly and full of heartfelt conviction—gripped the people of America. It emboldened us. It focused our attention heavenward. This great anthem of hope lifted our spirits during what was most certainly one of our nation's darkest hours.

Very quickly, that song spread like wildfire. That night, theaters on Broadway opened with "God Bless America." Its proud, emotion-charged lyrics rang out at the National Cathedral, the New York Stock Exchange, and virtually every sporting event in the land. Radio stations from rock to country watched as versions of "God Bless America" streaked to the top of their play lists.

In the months that followed, "God Bless America" became our nation's rallying cry. And why not? The song literally came alive on the Capitol steps and burned like a beacon over our land, harkening a nation back to its beginning—birthed under God as a great land of liberty. We know that our unprecedented political freedom, religious liberty, and economic prosperity are unusual. Few will deny someone or something has blessed our land. And on that terrible autumn day, this song reminded us that we would survive that trial and lead the world in this new century as long as we seek God's blessing.

Annette's Own Grassfire

Days after the tragedy, Annette received a Grassfire e-mail asking her to help encourage our leaders to make Irving Berlin's great song, "God Bless America," our national hymn—not our national anthem but our national hymn. We didn't set out to change or replace our national anthem, which holds such deep meaning for America. Instead, we wanted to recognize the role Berlin's song had played in our nation's recovery after 9/11. America should never forget 9/11, but as the years pass, our memory fades, making it imperative that we build memorials and tributes to key events. As the father of five, I don't want my children to forget that day. I hope decades from now our nation's students are learning about 9/11 and the important role "God Bless America" played in the days and months following that shocking day.

After reading the e-mail, Annette responded. She did something quite simple yet profound. She started her own grassfire on the Internet simply by e-mailing about fifteen of her friends, encouraging them to stand with her to make "God Bless America" our national hymn.

Instead of having *one* voice on this issue, Annette's voice began to grow as her friends received her e-mail and notified their friends. Soon, Annette had rallied ten others, then fifty, then one hundred. Annette's impact continued to grow and grow. When we caught up with Annette, 3,893 people had followed her lead and signed Grassfire's petition urging our leaders to recognize "God Bless America" as our national hymn.

"It's amazing to me," she told us. "I thought in my own mind that perhaps I could rally ten or fifteen people. I hadn't given a great deal of thought as to what would happen as those people e-mailed other people, and so on down the line."

Annette had just experienced the Grassfire Effect. Instead of one voice, Annette's voice had grown to nearly thirty-nine hundred voices. Until that time, the Internet was a convenient way for her to keep in touch with friends, do some shopping, or catch up on current events.

But in only a few minutes, her computer was transformed into something much more significant. It was a great center of activity whereby Annette—from her home in Florida—could rally a sizable brigade of citizens to take action on an issue without ever leaving her swivel chair.

Grassfire Effect Defined

In section 1 of this book, we explored the very genesis of ideas—how those sparks in our minds are fanned into full-fledged flames by focusing on people, setting goals, and plunging ahead into reality. Now the real fun begins because this is when the Grassfire Effect takes over and that flame turns into a full-fledged, world-changing grassfire!

So what exactly is the Grassfire Effect?

To put a fine point on it, the Grassfire Effect is "the inevitable result of your expanding circle of influence." Annette experienced it and so can you. This simple concept is the fundamental principle of growth for any individual or organization. This principle explains how the world is changed and how you can change your world. Why do some companies succeed? Check out their Grassfire Effect. Why do some individuals always seem to get more influence, more money, more of everything? Rest assured they have a very strong Grassfire Effect. Stated again:

The Grassfire Effect is the inevitable result of your expanding circle of influence.

In this section, we'll take a close look at these words so you can apply this principle on your job, with your unique idea, and in your life. I'll explain how Grassfire Economics can change the way you look at your own money and every business around you. You'll discover the one special ingredient that acts like gasoline poured on your grassfire. You will find out how to infuse everything you do—even the most menial tasks—with profound meaning and pur-pose. You'll find out how to practically apply the Grassfire Effect at work and in your community.

For example, let's say you want to change the garbage collection schedule in your neighborhood. You can write a letter to your city and even schedule a meeting with a city leader. But if you bring a letter signed by fifty of your neighbors that city leader will take even more notice. Ask those fifty neighbors to call that city leader over the next week and you might just get some action. That's the Grassfire Effect.

Grassfire Effect as a Life Principle

The Grassfire Effect can apply to any endeavor, any situation, any business, any organization. The principle can be found in the old proverb: "one can set a thousand to flight, two can set ten thousand." More important than your *one vote* on any particular matter is the unlimited potential of your influence on those around you, and the inevitable result that happens as your circle of influence expands.

Leaders always have a very high Grassfire Effect. Think of the president of the United States. Every word the president utters is measured and judged. A statement about the economy can send stocks tumbling. A phrase spoken out of context can set off an international incident thousands of miles away. This fact is amplified each elec-tion year as every word and action of a public official is parsed and dissected for political ammunition. Words that a political candidate say in a few brief moments can define an entire election.

The same is true for business leaders. Warren Buffett's comments on a particular company's potential reverberate in minutes across Wall Street. Buffett started as an infor-mal financial adviser for a close circle of friends. But his

Grassfire Effect began to grow, and now a single share of his Berkshire Hathaway stock sells for tens of thousands of dollars.

Leaders always have a very high Grassfire Effect, but here's the key that you need to understand to see your own Grassfire Effect take off: *you are a leader!* You have a circle of influence in your life that is impacted by what you say and do. It really does not matter how large that circle is. It could be just one person, but it's likely more than that. And if you will cultivate your Grassfire Effect, it will grow and your influence will inevitably expand.

Untold Story from Election 2000

A lack of understanding of the Grassfire Effect can breed apathy and cynicism. Those who see their lives in isolation can quickly wonder if their lone voice really matters. Perhaps this is why only 60 percent of eligible voters in America bother to vote. In political terms, they think they represent only one vote among millions. Does one vote really matter?

For many, the 2000 presidential election resolved that issue. Just a few hundred votes in Florida determined who would be president of the United States. In fact, it is quite possible that the 2000 presidential election was decided by a grassfire that began almost one year before the election, when a Cuban boy named Elian Gonzalez was found floating off the Florida coast in an inner tube. Elian's mother and other Cubans seeking refuge died, but the boy was rescued and taken in by his uncle in the Little Havana section of Miami.

For months, a high-profile debate ensued regarding whether Elian would stay in Florida or be returned to Cuba. Cuban Americans formed a human chain around Elian's uncle's house as reports surfaced that the government was planning to remove Elian from the home. Before dawn on Easter weekend, the Clinton administration authorized armed federal agents to forcibly take Elian. This predominantly Catholic Hispanic community was in the midst of its holiest of holidays — Holy Week. And then, the greatest trespass possible occurred during this sacred season. Who can forget the photograph of the armed federal trooper brandishing his automatic weapon and raiding the bedroom where Elian was sleeping?

Apparently, the Cuban Americans in Little Havana never forgot. That November, six in seven (86 percent) Cuban Americans in Miami-Dade County voted for George W. Bush, giving him the necessary margin of victory. Nationwide exit polling results show that 62 percent of Hispanics voted for Al Gore. Even in Bush's home state of Texas, Gore won the Hispanic vote 54 percent to 43 percent. Statewide in Florida, the Hispanic vote was evenly split (49 percent to Bush, 48 percent to Gore), but things were different in south Florida.

What about the recount in Miami-Dade, you ask? Didn't that recount prove that Gore would have won if the votes had been counted correctly? A closer look reveals how the Cuban American community was again the difference-maker. Of the 614 precincts in Miami-Dade, 135 precincts had been recounted, resulting in a net gain of 157 votes for Al Gore. This caused Democrats to extrapolate a 700-900 vote gain by Gore, which would have been more than enough votes to turn the election to Gore. But the recount was stopped.

Why was it stopped? Because the precincts which had been counted had overwhelmingly supported Gore (74 percent) as compared with Gore's county-wide advantage of 53 percent. Thus, the re-counters realized that Gore was not likely to make up anymore votes in precincts that favored Bush. Plus, the precincts of Little Havana were next to be counted and the Little Havana vote went overwhelmingly against Gore. The count stopped at the Little Havana precincts. Gore supporters to this day still talk authoritatively about the 700-900 vote swing that would have resulted from the recount, but the truth points to a grassfire in Little Havana.

Of course, there are certainly other factors to consider, but it is quite possible that the Grassfire Effect of a six-year-old Cuban boy's plight may well have swayed the delicate balance of the 2000 presidential election. The power of the grassfire!

The Screech and the Swift Boat

The Grassfire Effect was quite evident in the 2004 elections as well. Here are two examples. Howard Dean spent most of the preprimary season with a strong lead in the polls. Then came Iowa. It is possible that Dean could have survived John Kerry's surprising win in the nation's first caucus had it not been for that infamous "yeaaaaaahh" screech. Although it was quite unfair, it seemed the country found it difficult to take Dean seriously after the screech. It had a powerfully negative Grassfire Effect (a term we'll pursue in a few pages).

The 2004 election also featured a small group of Vietnam veterans forever known as the Swift Boat Vets for Truth. Whether you agree or disagree with the Swift Boat Vets, consider their amazing grassfire. In April 2004, a farmer from Iowa, a retired banker from Montana, a teacher from Kansas, and others (a few dozen vets in all) wanted to get out a message that challenged what Democratic nominee John Kerry was boasting about his activities in Vietnam. Seventeen of these vets traveled to Washington, D.C., and held a press conference to get their message out. Only C-SPAN covered the press briefing; the major media ignored their statements, except for a few shots off the bow from the *New York Times*.

These men felt their message needed to be heard by the American people but realized they would have to bypass the unresponsive traditional media by doing two things: writing a book and producing a television ad. With the book in development, they ran their ad on twenty stations with a pittance of a budget. That's when the Kerry campaign made a miscalculation, pressuring those stations to stop running the ads. The controversy that ensued launched a grassfire of historic political proportions.

According to John E. O'Neill, author of the Swift Boat Vets' book *Unfit for Command,* in only a few weeks more than seven in ten Americans had been exposed to the ad, thanks to the Grassfire Effect. This ad, along with subsequent ads, was downloaded four million times from their Web site, www.swiftvets.com. In all, $27 million was raised from more than 150,000 supporters across the country. The Swift Boat Vets conducted more than four thousand television and radio interviews. And the book hit number one on the *New York Times* best-seller list and has sold nearly 900,000 copies. It would be a gross simplification of the 2004 election to tie the outcome on election day to what the Swift Boat Vets did. Still, any history of that campaign must include what those men did.

O'Neill summarized his grassfire experience during the 2004 election: "The truth is an acorn that can grow into a mighty tree. And a small group of people, even amateurs, armed with the truth can sometimes be a mightier force than all of the forces of the mass media and big money in the United States."

An acorn that grows into a tree—I think of it as a spark that ignites a grassfire. That's what the Grassfire Effect is all about: turning one voice into hundreds of voices. Maybe it will impact an election or perhaps honor an inspiring song or even bring about change in the local government or school system.

That's our goal at Grassfire.org—to expand one voice into many voices of support for the issues we hold dear. But we take it one step further. Our desire is to enable people who are eager for results to actually *see* their own Grassfire Effect by letting them track how fast their impact is spreading. Our system lists how many people respond to their e-mails, the resulting "generations" of grassfire-spreaders who've caught the message and spread it to others, and even the states where their message is reaching. We have team members who reach tens of thousands of citizens in every state of the union — and they can actually *see* their Grassfire Effect!

The Other Side of the Grassfire-Effect Curve

At the end of the day, every business, every organization, and every leader must have a positive Grassfire Effect to sustain and grow its influence. That's because the Grassfire Effect works negatively in reverse. The negative Grassfire Effect is the inevitable result of your *shrinking* circle of influence.

Consider Sears and K-Mart. These two giants of the retail market have been supplanted by those guys in Bentonville, Arkansas—Wal-Mart. At some point for Sears and K-Mart, their Grassfire Effect turned upside down, and their customers started referring fewer and fewer customers. Their base began to shrink. Sears has seen its market share decline steadily in recent years. K-Mart began closing stores by the hundreds in an effort to recover from a bankruptcy reorganization. Ultimately, these two retail giants completed an $11-billion merger in an effort to reverse a negative Grassfire Effect.

Meanwhile, Wal-Mart's Grassfire Effect continues to grow. Today, Wal-Mart is the hub around which the entire retail market turns. But Wal-Mart's continued growth is not inevitable. If that company's Grassfire

Effect begins to shrink, no amount of advertising will be able to sustain its growth.

Your Family Grassfire

What if we apply the Grassfire Effect to other situations—like your family. Is your Grassfire Effect growing or shrinking with your spouse? How about your children? When the kids are young, you are the center of their universe. But if you do not plant the seeds—if you do not show them the love, care, concern, respect and attention they need when they are young—when they become teens your Grassfire Effect will be very small.

I view parenting as a graph with two lines: one represents the parent's authority and the other represents the parent's influence or Grassfire Effect. When a child is very young, the authority line is very high. As the child grows, the authority line drops until eventually the parent has no authority over the adult child. This is the natural process of raising children. The influence line, however, is not determined by the structure of the family but the strength of the relationship. Parents who invest in their children with their time, interest, love, discipline, prayers, tears, and joy open an account of influence in their kids that extends throughout each child's life. In fact, the parents' Grassfire Effect on their children can continue to grow throughout the lifetime of the relationship.

Your life's greatest potential Grassfire Effect is with your family. I think of my grandmother who didn't give up when her husband died, leaving her as an immigrant widow with two children to raise in New York City during the Depression. She would never see riches or be honored by the mayor. But she was faithful, and the Grassfire Effect of her life continues on to my children. I also think of how my mother-in-law often wears a sweatshirt that says, "I'm retired but I work part-time spoiling my grandchildren."

It's funny, but there's truth behind the joke. My mother- and father-in-law center their lives around their children and now their grandchildren. Their family Grassfire Effect will extend for generations to come.

Grassfire Effect with Friends and Neighbors

The Grassfire Effect works in friendships too. Think of the people you know who make the best friends. Chances are they have a lot of influence in the lives of their friends. And chances are they have that influence with quite a few people. That's because the Grassfire Effect is a life principle that applies equally to relationships as it does to commerce. An expanding circle of influence for you or your organization is the key to growth and success. It's what fuels grassfires and ultimately changes your world.

How about in your neighborhood? For generations of Americans, neighbors were nearly members of the family. This was especially the case in immigrant communities, such as the Bronx neighborhood my widowed grand- mother lived in during the Depression. During that trying time after my grandfather died, "Uncle Luther" (who was technically not related) helped Grandma find an apartment and land on her feet. He also pulled some strings to get my dad his first real job. Uncle Luther has long since passed away, and his act of kindness may have been all but for- gotten, but the Grassfire Effect of that simple act lives on in me and in my children.

The other day, I sat next to two dear ladies on a plane flight and found out they were eighty-three and ninety- two and had been neighbors for sixty-one years. I can only imagine how each of their lives has impacted the other through a friendship that has lasted most of the twentieth century and beyond. Today Americans live closer together than ever and have more communications technologies than ever, yet we still feel isolated in our suburban communities. If we move to another neighborhood, our current neighbors will hardly blink and not even bother to see us off.

Sure, it's nice to connect with people half a world away through the Internet. But it cannot replace a kind act from an Uncle Luther or a friendship that spans decades. So how's your neighborhood Grassfire Effect? Do you have a positive influence on your neighbors? Do they know your name? Do you know their names? Your neighborhood Grassfire Effect can start small—a plate of cookies or a helping hand—but it can have a profound impact.

Leadership Demands a Grassfire Effect

If you want to be a leader—if you want to influence and even *change* the world around you—then your life must develop a positive Grassfire Effect. And there is one way to do that: serve somebody. Service is love in action. Life is basically a grand love story on so many levels. And serving others is at the center of it all, including commerce, politics, family, career—you name it.

Search the pages of history, charting the lives of leaders who have had the most positive influence on society, and you will find one thing. Beyond those sparks of ideas that changed the world, beneath the dogged determination that turned their dreams into reality, you will find people who served their fellow man. Jesus said, "The greatest among you will be your servant" (Matt. 23:11). That's not cute religious thinking—that's the heart and soul of an expanding Grassfire Effect.

The next chapters will cover the economics behind this truth—that serving is the key to a thriving Grassfire Effect and why serving actually causes a greater Grassfire Effect. The principle is this: serving turns the focus of our efforts and energies back to people. When we serve, we touch the very heart of why we are on this earth, because life really is about people—*other* people. At my funeral, the part of me that will continue on is my investment in others—my investment in people.

That's what George Bailey discovered in the Christmas classic *It's a Wonderful Life*. George thought his life was a waste. His brother became a war hero. His friend made millions in plastics. The mean-spirited Mr. Potter seemed to compound his wealth despite his harsh, manipulative, and self-centered ways. Meanwhile, George—who always dreamed of traveling and changing the world—took on the duties of the eldest son and never left the small town where he was born. All he did was serve the people of Bedford Falls and care for his neighbors. When his Building and Loan ran into trouble, George despaired and wondered if life would have been better if he had never been born. That was when George was given the gift of seeing what life would have been like if he had never been born. He saw that the impact of his life had actually spread far and wide; dozens of people were directly affected by the spark of his life. He discovered that his life of loving people truly was a wonderful life. George Bailey had a powerful Grassfire Effect.

Most often, serving comes in small, humble doses—doing the things that others do not really want to do, meeting people's needs at a very basic level. For example, in the olden days of dusty streets and lots of walking, people had dirty feet. A very practical way to serve a visitor to your home was to wash their feet. In our world today, we wash feet only as a ceremony. But maybe there are modern-day equivalents, like mowing your neighbor's lawn or taking out their trash or trimming their hedges. When I was a resident adviser in college, I would often make the beds of the guys on our floor. It was somewhat unusual, but I guess it was a bit like feet washing. Want to have a grow-ing Grassfire Effect in your life that extends to your family, business, community, and even your world? Then make some beds. Mow a lawn. Wash some feet.

The Effect Comes with Patience

I call it a Grassfire *Effect* because *effect* speaks of a *result*. And in reality, the effect always is felt some time *after* the initial action. You may not see the effect immediately (Annette had no idea her influence was spreading), but the effect will come. Remember the definition? The Grassfire Effect is the inevitable *result* of your expanding (or shrinking) circle of influence.

If you are going to change your world, then you will need to identify some cause or agent that brings an increasing circle of influence to your life. That is the spark of an idea that we tracked in section 1 of this book. Take the spark, ignite a fire, and fan the flames. The rest—the Grassfire Effect—will follow. It may take generations (as in my grandmother's family), but it will happen.

But as I mentioned, it works both ways. The Grassfire Effect can work against you, your business, and your organization. And the difficult part is, when the Grassfire Effect starts working against you, you will not feel the effects immediately. Life will go on just fine, and you will be able to live off your prior positive Grassfire Effect for some duration of time. But it will catch up with you.

Maybe that's what is meant by a person's Peter Principle. The Peter Principle is the unofficial mantra of corporate life that says individuals are promoted to their level of incompetence. They end up in a position that, to their subordinates, they are obviously unqualified for. We often think of the Peter Principle as an inevitability of corporate life. But I disagree. I think the Peter Principle happens when an individual stunts his own personal growth and a negative Grassfire Effect sets in.

Grassfire.org has caused my personal Grassfire Effect to grow substantially. Today, on any given day, I can speak with more than one million citizens across the nation. From what were very small beginnings, Grassfire.org can activate tens of thousands of citizens at a moment's notice. I am also responsible for leading an organization that can handle this growth and move ahead into the future. I must deal with payrolls, budgets, expansion, and decisions that impact the direction of our organization.

Yet every day, I feel the warning signs that my Grassfire Effect could quickly begin shrinking and my Peter Principle will set in. It shows up in simple ways. Just the other day, I realized that my backlog of voice mails and e-mails was setting off a negative Grassfire Effect. If Grassfire.org is going to grow, then I must change my thinking and my structures to support the growth.

That is why one of the key areas that we stress at Grassfire is responding quickly to *all* e-mails from our online team members. Two of our staffers handle most of this correspondence responsibility, which can be overwhelming at times. I recall Ron telling me that he responded to 515 e-mails in one week—and that was a slow week! But he's committed to growing our grassfire— to building relationships with those people who have taken the time to write us.

Time and again, people are shocked that anyone even took time to reply to their message. We have won back countless friends through this process. And each e-mail serves to strengthen our Grassfire Effect. I may sound like a broken record about this, but it's so true. In business and in life, it's vital to maintain your Grassfire Effect by serving others.

A positive Grassfire Effect is a wonder. To see your influence growing exponentially is an amazing rush. I imagine Annette felt this when she realized her one voice had grown to nearly thirty-nine hundred. But a negative Grassfire Effect feels just the opposite. At first, what seemed so easy just becomes a bit more difficult—as if the currents in the ocean have shifted slightly, bumping you off those big waves. A few moments later you realize you are caught in a riptide. You are still swimming, but the shore is getting farther away. And then comes the critical moment: if you swim directly *against* the riptide, you will likely drown from sheer exhaustion. The only way to turn things around is to relax, chart a new course, and start swimming parallel to the beach. Likewise, you cannot determine to *reverse* a negative Grassfire Effect. You must *return* to those things that helped you find that Grassfire wave you used to be riding. Start swimming (i.e., *serving*) again. Churn up some fresh ideas. Start washing feet.

What Is Your Grassfire Effect?

What is your Grassfire Effect in your family? On the job? In your neighborhood? How about that idea of yours that you are developing, that spark of ingenuity to set off a Grassfire in your world? How can you put that spark in service to others so you can experience the wave of a Grassfire Effect?

As I write, Irving Berlin's "God Bless America" has yet to be added as our national hymn. But we're pressing on. After all, it was a small grassfire started by one man that led to the Pledge of Allegiance being adopted by our nation. The same is true of "The Star Spangled Banner."

As more time passes between 9/11 and today, we are more in need of benchmarks and memorials like "God Bless America" to take us back to that crucial time in our nation's history. How easily we forget what happened and why we must fight this global war on terror! That's why we will continue to work for "God Bless America" to be recognized as one of the memorials of 9/11. If you want to help, go to GodBlessHymn.com and sign our petition. Or, call your congressman right now and your two senators (call 202-224-3121 for the Capitol switchboard; just give them your zip code and they'll tell you who your representatives are) and tell them you support "God Bless America" being recognized as our national hymn.

Small sparks are fanned into flames by individuals who understand the Grassfire Effect. People like Annette, who used Grassfire's online system to light a wildfire that spread from one voice and has now grown to nearly four thousand voices! She's a modern-day George Bailey, and her impact on this one issue can be seen in tens of thousands of people. And I'm sure that Annette has a powerful Grassfire Effect with her family and friends on a host of topics. Annette is a world changer, and you can be as well as you expand your Grassfire Effect by serving others.

KEY EFFECTS

1. The Grassfire Effect is the inevitable result of your expanding circle of influence.

2. Grassfire Effect is a life principle of increasing influence that applies to individuals and organizations.

3. The Grassfire Effect causes businesses to grow and families to thrive.

4. The Grassfire Effect is a *result* that takes time and may take years.

5. Serving the needs of others is the key to a growing Grassfire Effect.

6. A negative Grassfire Effect is the result of your *shrinking* circle of influence.

FIRE STARTERS

🔥 On a scale of 1 to 10 (with 10 being the highest), rate your effectiveness in serving the following people:

___ your spouse

___ your children

___ your church or group

___ your coworkers

___ your neighbors

🔥 On a scale of 1 to 10 (with 10 being the highest), rate your Grassfire Effect with the following people:

___ your spouse

___ your children

___ your church or group

___ your coworkers

___ your neighbors

🔥 As your idea moves from spark to flame, your Grassfire Effect will be greatly determined by your ability to fill a need or provide a service. In one sentence, what need does your idea fulfill or what service does it perform?

_____

_____

_____

_____

_____

KEY INSIGHTS AHEAD:

- *What are the two ways to grow a business?*
- *Liberating wealth from physical things*
- *The basic question of economic theory*
- *Is the glass half full or half empty?*
- *Calculating your Grassfire Effect*

Chapter 7

Grassfire Economics
How Grassfires Grow Businesses

- There are only two ways to grow a business, organization, or church: You can buy customers or you can get them for free.
- Here's another thing: wealth is no longer tied to physical things. Real wealth is in the mind.
- What is the best measure of your business or organization's future success? Your Grassfire Effect.
- And by the way, the economic glass isn't half full or half empty. The real question is, how big a glass do you want?

Of course, I never heard these ideas in my college economics classes. I and countless others learned about macro theories and fiscal policy in school. But no one ever said I could buy customers or get them for free!

Basic Economic Theory

Interestingly, economic theory as a formal study is a relatively recent discipline in world history, developing in the seventeenth century as the world began to move from an agrarian to an industrial society. As a backdrop for understanding Grassfire Economics, I am going to summarize economic theory with three central questions:

Where does value (or wealth) reside, and is it fixed?

How is wealth distributed?

How does the market work?

Many theories have been offered to address the question of where wealth resides in an economy. Early theorists, called Mercantilists, believed that a nation's wealth was in physical resources such as gold and silver. Others thought agriculture was the primary measure of wealth because agriculture provided the essential resource for survival. Adam Smith's *Wealth of Nations* helped conceptualize the classical school of economic theory in which land, labor, and capital were viewed as the driving forces of a nation's wealth. Marxist economic thought believed the value of the economy did not rest in capital but in labor, what is called the labor theory of value. Where wealth resides is a crucial question; understanding the answer will help you unlock the Grassfire Effect.

The next basic question of economics is how wealth is distributed. Smith envisioned a free-market system in which buyers and sellers decided how wealth was distributed, regulated by the "Invisible Hand" of self-interested producers. Marxist economic thought rejected the invisible hand of the market, instead favoring central planning and government control of the means of production. In the twentieth century, economic theorists proposed various combinations of free-market and government planned systems. Please recognize that this is a massive simplification. Still, modern economic theory seeks to stabilize the economy through government intervention in various factors such as tax rates, government spending, deficit spending, and the money supply.

As for how the market actually works, there are three basic concepts: supply, demand, and equilibrium. Supply speaks of the provision of goods and services by the producers. Demand is what consumers are doing. Theorists wrestle over whether supply or demand is the driving force of the economy. In other words, does supply follow demand or does demand follow supply? The correct answer, of course, is yes! An increasing demand will result in more supply. An increase in supply can lower prices, which can increase demand which can raise prices, which can increase supply again. Suppliers can also create demand by introducing new products and services to the market. Equilibrium is the place at which the supply and demand curves meet. This is the market price for any commodity or service at a particular moment. Equilibrium is not static—it can fluctuate moment by moment. Perhaps the best case example is the stock market. Stocks on the open market post the last sell price (the equilibrium) along with the "bid" (demand) and "ask" (supply) prices. As buyers accept the ask, the price rises; as sellers accept the bid, the price falls.

The twentieth century saw the advent of approaches that focused on fiscal policy and government spending as the key stimulus for the market, especially in economic down times. Monetarists have instead looked to the supply of available money as the key indicator in the economy. Today, the Federal Reserve chairman is considered by some to be the most powerful man in America because he oversees bank reserve rates and interest rates. As interest rates drop, money becomes cheaper, and vice versa. Along the same lines, there remains much support for Arthur Laffer's Curve, which says cuts in tax rates actually can increase government tax revenues because people are left with more money to invest and spend.

Freeing Wealth from the Physical

Now let's tackle these three questions from the vantage point of Grassfire Economics.

First, where does wealth reside, or, more accurately, is wealth a fixed or growing resource? As I stated, when economists first began theorizing where wealth came from, many believed that true wealth was associated with physical commodities such as gold and other precious metals. While wealth will always at some level be tied to physical resources, it is clear we no longer live in the world of our forefathers. The physical world is much less limiting than it used to be. Man has tamed much of his environment, so that in the enterprising world basic survival needs are now in abundance. Very few people provide for their own basic necessities; we go to the supermarket. This is a dramatic shift from just a few hundred years ago. In recent decades, our freedom from the constraints of the physical world has increased dramatically. Cars and other modes of transportation allow us to choose where we live out of convenience instead of necessity. Planes have made the world a smaller place. Television brought the world to our living rooms, and now the Internet allows us to talk back to the world.

In the twenty-first century, wealth simply is not as dependent on physical resources. We live in what economic theorist George Gilder called the age of the microcosm—a time when the focus of power and knowledge is wrapped up in something about the size of your fingernail, the microprocessor. The tiny silicon chip that runs your computer, your cell phone, and dozens of other devices in your life is the most powerful tool in the world today.

And what is the essential raw material of the microchip and thereby the microcosm?

Beach sand.

Silicon is at its essence the same substance you walk on at the beach. And because beach sand and silicon are virtually unlimited resources, the "wealth" in the microcosm is no longer tied to physical resources. Where, then, is the wealth in the computer chip? It's in the mind of the person who made it. So wealth is no longer tied to physical things. Real wealth is in the mind.

Unleashing wealth from the strings of physical things makes some people nervous. They argue that our monetary system is really a mirage because it is no longer backed by gold and other commodities. They point out correctly that physical things, such as a manufacturing base for a nation, are still vitally important. They worry about building our economy on knowledge and information because you cannot eat information.

These are all good points worthy of consideration, but twenty-first-century citizens need not be alarmed that wealth is no longer tied to physical things for two relaxing reasons. First, tying wealth to physical things leads to a life philosophy that wealth is fixed and limited. There is only so much to go around. If you accept that there is only so much to go around, the prime concern becomes not the creation of wealth but the *distribution* of wealth.

In fact there are only two economic schools of thought: one focuses on the *creation* of wealth and the other on the *distribution* of wealth. If wealth is fixed, then we all should be primarily concerned with how that fixed pool of wealth is disbursed. This is called the zero-sum game, but I'm not sure why it is called a game because no one wins.

Focusing on the distribution of wealth weakens individuals, families, communities, and nations. It creates envy and undermines property rights. Ultimately, it breeds dependency on the distributors (i.e., the government), while creating a lower class that is trained to feed off of others. And because politicians control the process of distribution, the political class is greatly empowered in our society. In the past fifty years, judges have gotten into the game of distribution, further establishing their authority over our lives.

Call it what you want, but it's Marxism by another name. If you focus on the distribution of wealth, you lose sight of the true source of wealth and economic growth, and you will stunt or stop altogether your personal grassfire.

Wealth *Ex Nihilo*

The second reason you can relax in seeing real wealth beyond the physical world is because that is the way it was *in the beginning*.

As discussed in chapter 2, the creative impulse in man—the ability to reason and choose and invent and create—is what makes us most human. Why? Because we are image-bearers of the Creator who made the world *ex nihilo*, which means "out of nothing." In Grassfire Economics, the human mind is capable of unlimited ingenuity and inventiveness. Real wealth has always been in the mind of man.

The other day, I was driving in my car with one of my daughters and a world-opening opportunity suddenly was upon us. I was complimenting Hope on her test scores from the school year. I then told her that she was among the brightest minds of her age group in the country and even in the world. I said she certainly could be one of the people who make breakthrough inventions that change the world. She looked at me both puzzled and obviously doubtful of what I said.

I then asked her if she thought cars, TVs, and cell phones would look the same in ten years. The answer was obvious to her. She was only nine but had already seen TVs, computers, and cell phones change dramatically. Kids today easily accept new technologies as a matter of course, almost as if anything is possible. For example, I hooked up a digital video recording (DVR) system to our television recently, and it took minutes for my kids to adapt to pausing, rewinding, and recording live television. I've talked up DVRs to friends my age and they instinctively resist. The adaptability of "millennials" to technological change is remarkable and a marked change from just one generation ago. But kids today still need to apply this change-embracing worldview to *their* world. My discussion with Hope was important because I believe it began a transition in her thinking. Yes, the world will change. More important, it is possible that *she* will be one of the world changers.

Motivational speakers often use the mythological story of Charles Duell, the U.S. commissioner of patents who supposedly resigned in 1899, saying that "everything that can be invented has been invented." No evidence exists that this patent official ever made such a statement, but this urban legend lives on because that kind of thinking sneaks into each of our minds on occasion. It's time to reject any such thoughts. As I write, I'm sitting at my dining room table with a computer no more than three-fourths of an inch thick outfitted with wireless technology that connects me at a moment's notice to virtually any place in the world. I can carry my computer to the den and still surf the Web. This computer has the equivalent of an advanced banking system, a desktop publishing platform, a music-recording mixing board, a powerhouse database, a complex contact management system, a DVD burner, a digital video studio, and much more built right into it. And it will be old in two years, truly obsolete in five.

"Open Source" Creativity

Interestingly, the rate of new inventions as measured by the patent office has declined in recent years. But creativity is not in decline. A better analysis may be that change is happening so fast that companies may be relying less and less on the formal patent concept to secure their new ideas. The best protection is to keep your core ideas in secrecy as long as possible and continue to develop new ideas along the way.

To see how fast the world is changing, consider the open source-coding revolution in which the source coding of software is openly shared. The benefit of this method is best explained by opensource.org: "When programmers can read, redistribute, and modify the source code for a piece of software, the software evolves. People improve it, people adapt it, people fix bugs. And this can happen at a speed that, if one is used to the slow pace of conventional software development, seems astonishing."

I would tweak this definition's use of the word *evolves*. This is not a chance-driven process. Unlike evolution, there is a mind (or in this case thousands of minds) driving the growth and development of the software. It is much more like a grassfire in that the open-source environment allows programmers around the world to fan the flames of software development. Open source-coding creates a high-tech grassfire.

Your mind is your greatest asset. It is your greatest resource. It is the engine of unlimited ideas and has the potential for great wealth—not *redistributing* wealth from someone else but actually *creating* wealth by adding value to even the most ordinary of elements like beach sand. The next time you go to the beach, grab a handful of sand and realize that the human mind has turned that limitless resource into untold wealth. And that's the way the world is supposed to be: creativity *ex nihilo*.

When Will We Run Out of Oil?

Here's another example of how resources are not fixed and that wealth is in ideas. If you were born before 1965, you probably remember the oil crisis of the 1970s. While I was in middle school, during the height of the oil crisis and the long lines at the gas stations, we had an "expert" talk to us students about the oil crisis. He told us that the world's oil reserves were nearly used up. He told us we only had twenty years left before oil supplies would be exhausted. And that was optimistic.

I was about twelve at the time and can remember being a bit afraid because twenty years was certainly within my lifetime. We wouldn't even make it to the year 2000 based on this gloomy projection. The presenter also said nuclear power was a poor choice. Solar and wind power were offered as bright hopes for tomorrow. In the meantime, he said, we must conserve, and with luck we could extend those reserves a few years while scientists desperately work to avoid total catastrophe.

This was bad news for the world but good news for the environmentalists in the 1970s, who saw the fossil fuel-burning internal combustion engine as the enemy of the environment. Yet the environmentalists were not alone in the analysis of the oil supply. In 1879, just twenty years after oil was first struck in America, the U.S. Geological Society was formed in part out of a concern for oil supplies. By 1919 *Scientific American* was stating that only twenty years of oil supply remained. And in 1920, while experts were estimating U.S. oil reserves at 6.7 billion barrels, a *National Geographic* article on oil supply was subtitled, "Where will our children get [oil] when American wells cease to flow?"

But something shocking happened over the next eighty years—oil reserves actually climbed despite increasing demand. Dr. Bill Kovarik, professor at Radford University, has studied what he calls the "Oil Reserve Fallacy" extensively and has constructed a timeline that shows by 1950 world oil reserves were estimated at 100 billion barrels. But over the next thirty years, world oil reserves did something shocking—reserves climbed. By 1980, proven oil reserves worldwide stood at an estimated 648 billion barrels. By 1993, estimated reserves stood at 999 billion and grew to 1,016 billion in 2000.

Today, the estimate of total world oil endowment (proven and unproven) is 3 *trillion* barrels, a 500 percent increase over the estimated world oil endowment only fifty years ago. It should also be noted that these numbers do not include shale oil, of which there is an estimated 15 trillion barrels worldwide. With shale oil, it is reasonable to say that the world has five hundred years of oil supply. And that's what we know now. We should not be surprised if the estimated total world oil endowment grows again by fivefold in the next fifty years. It is safe to say the world will not run out of oil for quite some time—certainly not before oil becomes obsolete and the current debate is long forgotten.

Why is the supply of proven oil reserves increasing? Two main factors: Technological advances have given man access to oil fields that could not be tapped a few decades ago. Also, as the market price of oil increases, it becomes cost-effective to use more expensive oil-extracting techniques, putting more potential oil reserves within reach.

There could be a third factor. We have been told that oil is the end result of a long process that took place millions of years ago in which plant life decomposed and was pressurized. Here's how the Web site schoolscience.co.uk describes the process: "Tiny animals and plants that live in the sea are called plankton. The plankton that lived in the Jurassic period made our crude oil. When they died they sank to the bottom and slowly got buried by sand and mud. Over millions of years, the dead animals and plants got buried deeper and deeper. The heat and pressure gradually turned the mud into rock and the dead animals and plants into oil and gas."

This is the same script I learned in public schools in the 1970s. According to this theory (which, by the way, is not presented as a theory but as an absolute fact as if someone was there to witness this process millions of years ago), if it takes millions of years for oil to be created, and man is using about 80 million barrels *every single day* (enough to fill forty football stadiums), it seems logical to assume the supply is running out. As I have shown, we have been working on the premise of oil scarcity basically since the first oil well was drilled 150 years ago. But oil isn't running out. Oil reserves are increasing, which we assume is because our technology allows us to find more oil.

But could it be something else altogether? In 2004, it was reported that some oil fields located in the Gulf of New Mexico appeared to be refilling. This is a startling phenomenon. Another fascinating point is that oil and natural gases are being discovered at much greater depths than would be expected given the prevailing theory of how fossil fuels were created. This is leading some scientists to rethink the theory of the origin of so-called fossil fuels. Some are considering that such fuels are actually the by-product of deposits of methane that have been in the earth since the planet was formed.

The late Thomas Gold, a distinguished professor at Cornell University, championed this theory and formulated his ideas in the book *The Deep Hot Biosphere*. If this theory is true, it may be virtually impossible to exhaust the supply of "fossil" fuels. And even if fossil fuels were to somehow run out in hundreds of years, man's creativity and ingenuity would certainly have developed a new, more abundant source of fuel.

The potential of a possibly unlimited supply of fuel is not good news to the doomsayers who believe that the internal combustion engine is what Al Gore called a "mortal threat" to humankind. But the news of increasing fuel reserves has not stopped the doomsayers; it has just changed their strategy. They have turned their attention from conservation to something much more ominous—the destruction of the ozone layer, global warming, and, once again, total world catastrophe.

What does this have to do with economics? Quite a bit. One's economic theory is greatly influenced by one's world-view. Marxism was an outgrowth of Darwinism—a materialistic worldview that says all that exists is the material world. Marx believed that economies would evolve and make capitalism obsolete. Contrast materialism with the belief in a Creator who creates *out of nothing*—the material world is not the beginning nor the end. And this Creator has imprinted human beings with enough of His nature so that humans can create in their minds.

The Globesity Scare

One more example to challenge your thinking on resource limitations: in 2004, the World Health Organization launched a major campaign to fight the global obesity epidemic. The WHO Web site reported, "An escalating global epidemic of overweight and obesity— 'globesity'—is taking over many parts of the world." According to the WHO, the estimated number of obese people rose from 200 million in 1995 to 300 million in 2000. That's a 50-percent increase in just five years. Extrapolate that rate and there will be one billion obese people in 2015. In less than fifty years, at that same growth rate, globesity will certainly be on everyone's mind because *everyone on the planet will be obese!* I'm poking fun, but it is interesting to note that in 2004, the WHO said there are more obese people in the world than hungry people.

It's getting harder and harder to believe in the limited-resources theory. It's time to stop apologizing for the fact that the United States is far and away the world's largest consumer of resources. It's time to stop feeling guilty because we throw away more food than some countries eat. Instead, our position should be that the entire world should be so prosperous and innovative that their citizens will be consuming resources in abundance. In Grassfire Economics, the economic glass isn't half full or half empty. The real question is, how big a glass do you want?

Supersize It!

This principle of Grassfire Economics applies both to the global (macro) world as well as to your personal (micro) world—your personal life, your family, your business, your organization, your idea.

How large a glass do you want? Is it any wonder that America is the country that invented the supersized combo meal? I recently ran into a friend who was toting this super-duper-sized insulated refillable drink cup that he picked up at a convenience store. It was an unbelievable cup—probably ninety-eight ounces. And it's a symbol of the American way that we should embrace. Sadly, many people who supersize their drinks are too willing to settle for an eight-ounce cup for their personal dreams. How about you? Forget if your glass is half full or half empty and work on getting a bigger glass. Toss that eight-ounce cup of limited dreams and supersize your goals. That's Grassfire Economics—a view of the world in which a tiny spark of an idea can spread rapidly and grow larger than you dare to think or imagine.

How to Grow Your Business

One more aspect of Grassfire Economics must be grasped to get the full picture. At the beginning of this chapter, I proposed that there were really only two ways to grow any business, organization, or church: You can buy customers or you can get them for free.

It's really that simple. A business needs customers. An organization or a church needs constituents. Two essential terms that will further your understanding of this concept are *acquisition cost* and *lifetime value of a customer.* Acquisition cost refers to your cost to acquire a new customer. This is the great challenge of any business or organization— acquiring new customers. Lifetime value refers to just that—the customer's value in his lifetime to your business or organization. The higher the lifetime value of a customer, the higher the acquisition cost that can be justified.

Consider nonprofit organizations, many of which will invest sixty dollars or more to find a new supporter, because they know that on average that same supporter will donate four hundred dollars to the organization over that donor's "lifetime." The organization will build a plan to break even on the sixty-dollar investment in the first six to nine months. The same applies to for-profit businesses. Some churches use this same thinking to decide how much to spend on advertising and other membership-growth programs.

So every company and organization that advertises or invests resources in finding new customers is "buying" customers for a price. There is only one other option and that is to get customers for free. But how do you do that?

It's simple—have your customers find customers for you. Many sole-proprietorships rely entirely on this method. They do not invest in advertising or direct-mail marketing. Instead, they trust that their customers will refer them to other customers. In the simplest terms, this is concept of the Grassfire Effect (the inevitable result of your expanding circle of influence).

Measuring Your Grassfire Effect

But the Grassfire Effect is not just a concept: it is a practical measurement that can help you chart your company's or organization's success and growth. At Grassfire.org, all of our efforts are totally dependent on grassroots citizens taking action and rallying their friends. We have rallied hundreds of thousands of citizens on key issues without spamming. If someone receives a Grassfire.org e-mail from us it is because they signed one of our petitions or visited our Web site. Only as friends refer friends do we see these large online constituencies on key issues develop. So we watch to see how many referrals are signing and actually measure the Grassfire Effect of that issue to determine just how *hot* a particular issue really is.

Every individual, every family, every business, every church, and every organization has a Grassfire Effect. Every business or organization should have as part of its vital statistics a precise measure of its Grassfire Effect. The Grassfire Effect should be tracked by CEOs more closely than profit margins or stock prices. Each organization will need to find the best way to measure its Grassfire Effect. But at the end of the day, here's the best indicator:

Does the average person coming in contact with you or your organization cause your influence to expand or shrink?

More specifically, how many customers on average does each customer bring to your store? See it as an equation:

Grassfire Effect = referred customers / existing customers

$$GE = RC/EC$$

Let's say you calculate that 523 referral customers came to your furniture shop and purchased furniture in a year. At the beginning of the year you had 650 customers. Your Grassfire Effect would be .81 (because 523/650 = .81). That means each of your customers "gave" you .81 additional customers. Let's say the average furniture store customer nets your company $200. That means the average customer actually is bringing an additional $162 in referrals.

Why is the Grassfire Effect important to know? It can help you plan your marketing and business growth in many ways. For example, let's say you want to offer your customers some bonus for referrals. Your Grassfire Effect tells you how much you can invest. A measure of a Grassfire Effect also impacts how many customers your company can afford to purchase through advertising and other means. If each purchased customer is going to generate .81 other customers, you might be able to justify spending more on purchasing customers.

Mixing Free and Paid Customers

Take a look at the fastest-growing companies in the past twenty years and you will find that each had extraordinarily high Grassfire Effects. Buying customers creates linear growth—you get the customers you pay for. The Grassfire Effect is the only way to grow exponentially.

Need a Grassfire Effect example from your own life? Here you go: Do you use the Google search engine? Why? I doubt you saw an advertisement for Google. Most likely a friend e-mailed you something from Google or told you about something he found on Google, and you said, "What's Google?" A few years ago, a friend told me about Google, and I've steered dozens of people to Google, all of them free customers, contributing to Google's exponential growth in the early part of this decade.

But the key is not just to try for free customers—the key is to increase your Grassfire Effect measures and then leverage your Grassfire Effect to make all your customers more valuable to your company. In fact, the best models combine a paid-customer strategy with a free-customer strategy. Even if you have a strong Grassfire Effect, you should still consider buying customers. Avoid the mistake that many successful small businesses make. Take Barry the Plumber. Barry does just fine because his friends refer enough work to keep him very busy. Barry the Plumber then mistakenly turns his nose up at advertising and other methods of buying customers. He feels like it's somehow dirty. But what if Barry bought some customers and then put his good name—his Grassfire Effect—to work? His business could grow rapidly with respectable referrals.

For a big company like Wal-Mart, many new customers are a hybrid of paid and free. Maybe the new customer saw the Wal-Mart ads, got the flyer in the newspaper, and then decided to go to the store when a friend mentioned something he bought. That's a hybrid situation—a powerful blend of free and paid strategies at work. But remember, Wal-Mart's growth is not inevitable. If Wal-Mart's Grassfire Effect goes negative, even a multi-million-dollar advertising budget that is "buying" customers will not be enough to stop the hemorrhaging. A negative Grassfire Effect will kill even Wal-Mart. That is why your company's Grassfire Effect gives you a window into your company's future.

The Grassfire Quotient

In theory, if you have a Grassfire Effect of 1.0, that means one customer will bring you one customer on average per year. In theory, your customer base could double in only one year. But there is another factor that needs to be considered: attrition. Attrition, or customers you lose, is a fact of life for any organization. Attrition is a separate measure although it undoubtedly impacts your Grassfire Effect. Even if your organization has a high Grassfire Effect, you will have some attrition. If you have high attrition, your customers will be leaving instead of finding new customers, and your Grassfire Effect will be lowered.

To sustain growth, your mix will include customers you buy, free customers, and customers you lose. Taken together, we call this the Grassfire Quotient—an overall measure of how your customer base is growing.

Grassfire Quotient = (purchased customers + referred customers − lost customers)/existing customers

$$GQ = (PC + RC - LC)/EC$$

If your Grassfire Quotient is 1.0, your customer base will grow by 100 percent annually. As long as your Quotient is positive, your organization is growing. If it drops below zero, your customer base is shrinking.

The Grassfire Quotient is not a measure of your company's profitability or its financial growth; it measures how your customer base is doing—growing or shrinking? It is possible to show higher profits in a year in which your Grassfire Quotient actually is a negative number, indicating that your customer base is shrinking. That's because the Grassfire Quotient does not factor in the profitability of each customer. For example, your company could face a cash crunch and decide it "can't afford" to purchase new customers this year (i.e., your company stops advertising). Because the profit margin on new customers is less than on existing customers, your profit may increase in the short term. But a negative Grassfire Quotient will indicate that tough times are ahead as your customer base shrinks.

Grassfire Economics is a way to view your world and understand the economic engine of the Grassfire Effect. What is your fundamental economic philosophy? Do you see wealth and resources as limited or unlimited? What about that glass that is holding your life and your idea—is it half full, half empty, or not big enough? Think through the two basic ways to grow any business or organization. What is your current mix? Are you relying on paid customers or free customers? And how would you calculate your Grassfire Effect? You may not learn this in business school, but this fundamental principle of organizational growth will unlock the potential for exponential growth in your personal Grassfire.

KEY EFFECTS

✓1. There are two ways to grow a business: buy customers or get them for free.

✓2. A fundamental question of economic theory is whether wealth is created or just redistributed. Your answer will determine your grassfire's potential.

✓3. Wealth is no longer tied to physical things; wealth is in the mind.

✓4. The Grassfire Effect is a key business measure, calculated by dividing total referred customers by existing customers: GE = RC/EC.

✓5. The Grassfire Quotient is an overall measure of how a company's customer base is growing: GQ = (PC + RC-LC)/EC.

✓6. Every business and organization should track its Grassfire Effect and Grassfire Quotient as key measures of future growth.

FIRE STARTERS

🔥 Before you read this chapter, did you believe the pool of wealth was fixed or growing? What did you think was more important: wealth distribution or wealth creation? Describe your economic view *before* you read this chapter.

_____

_____

🔥 Think of three examples of how wealth is more a matter of mind than matter:

1.

2.

3.

🔥 Estimate the Grassfire Effect of your business or organization:

Annual Referred Customers (RC): _____

Total Existing Customers (EC): _____

Grassfire Effect: RC/EC = _____

Chapter 8

Grassfire Effectors

Practical Tools to Increase Free Business

I thought you guys were crooks."

It was one of the nicest things anyone had ever said to our Grassfire team. Here's why.

Mr. Smith, a long-time Grassfire team member, was quite angry. In fact, he was mad enough to send us several hostile, unprintable e-mails. Why? Because he was certain that he had made a donation to Grassfire and wanted to get the special premium gift we had offered. Weeks had passed and no gift had arrived.

Those angry e-mails filtered to our order-processing department where our staff searched diligently for Mr. Smith's order, hunting for any record of a credit card transaction or a processed check. We found nothing.

At that point, we had two choices: tell Mr. Smith that we had no record of the transaction and that he would have to send us proof (and after his profanity-laced tirade, that was our first impulse) or send Mr. Smith the special gifts he thought he was due. We chose the latter option, sending him the gifts along with a few other items our staff threw into the bag. We e-mailed him to say that we could not find a record of his transaction but were sending him the premium gifts anyway.

A few days later, Mr. Smith received a packet of goodies. It must have felt like Christmas because he immediately wrote us one of the nicest apology letters we have ever received.

This story illustrates many of the pointers that help to grow your Grassfire Effect and increase your company's free business. In total, six "Grassfire Effectors" can enhance your relationship with your customers and increase your Grassfire Effect. We'll first learn about them, then discover how Grassfire Meetings can engage your employees in the process of growing your Grassfire Effect.

Is the Customer Always Right?

Is it true that the customer is always right? That idea works great in theory, but in practice when customers are cursing you out for something you didn't do the customer is flat-out wrong!

The reason we say that the customer is always right is because the customer controls your Grassfire Effect. Every customer who walks in your door, visits your church, sends a kid to your school, or donates to your organization will have an impact on your Grassfire Effect.

But the customer isn't always right. In fact, as in the case of our Mr. Smith, the customer can be dead wrong. But "right and wrong" is the wrong way to be thinking if you're thinking customer service. Right and wrong puts you and your customer on opposite sides of a fence. Instead of thinking, *The customer is always right*, it would be better to think, *The customer is always . . . Mom.*

If you saw your mom's face every time someone interacted with your business, you would treat your customers differently. After all, mom gave birth to us and nurtured us from our infancy, giving us a built-in respect for her. So that's the first tip to increasing your Grassfire Effect: seeing Mom in every customer. Print off these words and put them in a place where your team can see them:

GRASSFIRE EFFECTOR NO.1—
THE CUSTOMER IS ALWAYS MOM!

Breaking Down the Anonymity

But even the Mom mind-set will fall short from time to time due to the anonymity of the people we interact with on a daily basis.

I live in a sizable metropolitan area—a military town often touted as the largest city that doesn't have a major league sports team—and it's big enough that I rarely run into anyone I know while shopping. In fact, if I run into someone I know at the grocery store, it's almost cause for a small party in aisle 2. "Hey, Fred! What a bizarre coincidence to meet right here in the frozen food section. What are the chances of that?"

When I buy a chicken sandwich at a fast-food place, I deal with a total stranger. I pull up to the drive-thru window, give my order, trade money for my sandwich, check for mayo, then drive away. If my fast-food server died in a car accident twenty-four hours after she delivered me a fresh chicken sandwich, not only would it not affect me; I would likely never know. The chicken-sandwich maker's life doesn't matter to me unless it interferes with my order. Even though the sandwich maker is dead, I can still go back to the sandwich shop the next day as if nothing happened.

Does that make me a heartless monster who is so obsessed with his own needs—in this case, a chicken sandwich—that I care not for my fellow human beings? Perhaps. But let's paint another scenario.

What if a really good friend of mine works the drive-thru at the sandwich shop? I pull up to her window and order a chicken sandwich. My friend smiles at me and hands me a chicken sandwich.

"Susan!" I say.

"Hey, Steve!" she replies. "How're Stacy and the kids?"

"They're doing great. How's Tony?"

"He's out of town this week, but we're doing great."

I look at the sandwich bag and shake my drink. "Would you mind getting me some mayo, and I hate to trouble you, but could I get a little less ice in this cup if it's not a problem?"

"Sure! No problem. Here you go. See you Sunday at church!"

I drive away with my chicken sandwich, thinking about what a wonderful time I had in that drive-thru lane. Later that evening, I get a chilling phone call—Susan died in a car accident after work. I rush to Tony's house. I'm in shock for days. What was different? It was the same sandwich, the same service, the same everything, except one thing—I knew Susan.

Anonymity is the enemy of customer service. Anonymity will weaken your Grassfire Effect, so break down the anonymity every chance you get. The best place to start is with that first gift your parents gave you—your name.

Destroying anonymity begins with getting to know someone's name. That is why retailers and restaurants have their servers wear name tags. At some stores, cashiers are required to give you one dollar instantly if they do not thank you *by name*. "Thank you, Mr. Elliott, for shopping here." A really good bank will get to know your name right away so that tellers can recognize you as you walk in the door. I love my bank because tellers always say, "Hi, Mr. Elliott!" It still shocks me just a bit, but I like it. *Wow! Someone in the world knows me. I think I'll come back here.*

GRASSFIRE EFFECTOR NO.2—
LEARN YOUR CUSTOMER'S NAME

If you want to have a positive Grassfire Effect, take hold of this truth: Every relationship begins with a name. You really cannot know people at all until you know their names. It's a homing beacon for our souls. We stand at attention when someone says our name. But the proper order of things is always to *give* first. That's why you should always offer your name first.

Consider Alcoholics Anonymous. The biggest barrier to overcoming alcoholism is for the alcoholic to admit to the disease. The newcomer sits by and watches as others like him stand up and share, leading off with their first names. The newcomer begins to identify with others who share his problem—real people with names who are stepping out from the shame. The healing begins when an anonymous soul stands up before the group and says, "I'm Steve and I'm an alcoholic."

The Wal-Mart Greeter

The name exchange is just the first step to breaking down the anonymity barrier. Your organization also needs to adapt a small-town mind-set. It really is impossible to understand or appreciate Grassfire.org without visiting the small town in Iowa where our offices are located— Maxwell, Iowa—the Mayberry-without-the-traffic town where Bob lives. There are no traffic lights. People do not bother to lock their car doors. Our office sits next to the general store. It's a store that is straight out of a storybook.

Run by two brothers, you enter through a creaky old door. The decades-old wooden floor has tracks worn down the three or four aisles. The walls are lined with memorabilia from years gone by. One of the brothers is generally at the entrance, greeting customers; the other stays toward the back at the deli counter. But these aren't customers—they are friends and neighbors and an occasional new face. All get the same welcome. Every day around lunchtime, kids from the high school stream over for deli sandwiches. Our staff walks over and puts in their orders, which are added to a running tab that is reconciled about once a month or so.

Even though our online team consists of more than one million people, our Grassfire team still operates as if it's that general store. That's because our team simply cannot live any other way—that's how you live in a small town. That's why Mr. Smith got extra stuff in the mail from our team. And that's why our employees have regular dialogues by e-mail with as many team members as is possible. Grassfire.org is a "small town" that happens to consist of more than one million people.

GRASSFIRE EFFECTOR NO. 3—
MAKE YOUR BUSINESS A "SMALL TOWN"

In 1980, Wal-Mart founder Sam Walton visited a Wal-Mart in Louisiana and noticed an employee greeting people at the door. He liked the idea so much that he decided to implement it at every Wal-Mart. The people-greeter program is all about creating that first impression of a friendly, warm environment—a small-town environment—that you will want to come back to *and* refer your friends to. Consider the genius of the idea: Wal-Mart's biggest criticism continues to be that it is the corporate giant that comes into town and puts many local merchants out of business—the grocer, the neighborhood pharmacy, hardware store, clothing retailers, and so on. But standing there at the entrance to your local Wal-Mart is a friendly neighbor, usually an elderly member of your community, with an extended hand, a smile, a yellow sticker for kids and a friendly "Welcome to Wal-Mart!" Wal-Mart has an estimated thirty thousand people-greeters. That's an investment of millions of dollars annually in a greeter program.

Another aspect of Wal-Mart's small-town philosophy is called the Ten-Foot Rule. Early in the days of Wal-Mart, Sam Walton would challenge Wal-Mart associates with these words: "I want you to promise that whenever you come within ten feet of a customer, you will look him in the eye, greet him, and ask him if you can help him."

Today, Wal-Mart still upholds the Ten-Foot Rule, which goes a long way in turning the world's largest business into a small-town neighborhood store. The question for your business isn't whether you can afford to create a small-town atmosphere; it's whether you can afford *not* to make your business a small town.

Reaching the Opinion Leaders

Technology now allows companies to gather massive amounts of information on customers. When I call some companies, the caller-ID technology automatically accesses my database file, and the phone operator greets me with "Hello, Mr. Elliott, would you like to order a large pepperoni pizza again?" It is an impressive customer service strategy.

But sadly, the power of technology is weakening the power of knowing someone's name. Even in a midsized business, you cannot know all your customers personally. It's really the computer that knows my name. That is why it is still important for you and the members of your organization to recognize that, no matter how big or small your organization is, you will always have an inner circle of people. The question is, who should be in the inner circle? For the answer, we go to the 80/20 Rule, also known as Pareto's Principle. Credited to an Italian economist, Vilfredo Pareto, this principle states that 20 percent of the people do 80 percent of the work. This is a truism that works in most settings. Applied to the Grassfire Effect, 20 percent of your customers will determine 80 percent of your Grassfire Effect.

But how do you find those 20 percent—the people I call the Opinion Leaders? The Opinion Leaders are those who have a disproportionate share of the influence on your organization. Therefore, the Opinion Leaders should receive a disproportionate share of your attention. You should actively seek to draw Opinion Leaders into your inner circle.

GRASSFIRE EFFECTOR NO. 4— CULTIVATE OPINION LEADERS

Author Malcolm Gladwell has developed an interesting approach to finding Opinion Leaders in his work, *The Tipping Point*. Gladwell identifies three types of people who have the most influence on the growth of your organization: salesman, connectors, and mavens. Salesmen do just what the term implies—they find something they like and then use their persuasive abilities to convince other people to try the new thing. It is their persuasive abilities that drive the show, not their deep relationships or their knowledge of the issue.

The second type of opinion leader identified in *The Tipping Point* is the connector. The connector is the person who seems to know everyone and is always bringing people together. They are life's matchmakers. Connectors can connect you to the right people who will grow your business.

The third type is called the maven, who serves as an ombudsman. The person who started *Consumer Reports* is probably a maven. Mavens will fact-check everything, enjoying the painstaking investigation and the confidence that comes from their knowledge. They then share that knowledge not to be known for their prowess but so that others will be in the know. Mavens are looking for the snakes in the grass, and when they find a snake, they let the world know.

Gladwell says a good business will build "traps" to identify and cultivate salesmen, connectors, and mavens. He uses the example of the toll-free "comments" phone number printed on Ivory soap. Why would someone have a comment on the blandest, plainest, most basic soap in the world? The question isn't *why* but *who*. And that *who* is a maven. The comments line is a maven trap.

As I have noted, our Grassfire system tracks the personal impact of every Grassfire team member. We know for a fact that the 80/20 Rule works at Grassfire—20 percent of our team members rally 80 percent of our support base. By its nature, our system identifies the salesmen and the connectors. Internally, we call our most active team members "superactivists." We also answer thousands of e-mails from our team members. Many of these e-mails come from the mavens of our group. We joke that we don't have to proofread our copy because, within minutes of sending an update, a maven will tell us how we erred. On a more serious note, our mavens tell us when something has really gone wrong, often before our own staff discovers it. The mavens have saved us from real problems many times, and they also give us many of our best new ideas.

The 80/20 Rule is operating right now at your organization. Twenty percent of your customers are likely determining 80 percent of your Grassfire Effect. These are your Opinion Leaders, and to maximize your Grassfire Effect, you need to find ways in your business to cultivate these leaders.

Brand Yourself!

At the end of the day, your Grassfire Effect is dependent on your customers or constituents taking ownership of your business or organization. I'm not necessarily talking about actual ownership (although that is one very good way to create this vested interest in your organization). The best kind of customer "ownership" is at the most basic level—the level of communication. Consider this: language is the first way that we take ownership of the world. One of the first words babies learn (especially babies with older siblings) is *mine*. We assign words to the things we own, and we take ownership of our world through language.

In marketing terms, it's called branding. Branding is the ultimate step in ownership. Consider the following choices:

Coke or Pepsi?

Mac or PC?

Nike or Reebok?

Old Navy or Gap?

Chances are, you identify with and prefer one choice over the other. I like Pepsi and when I think of cola, my mind actually frames the word *Pepsi* inside my head. I'm wired for Pepsi. At the end of the day, I *own* Pepsi. How did this happen? I would contend that Pepsi tastes better, but if I'm honest, somehow my taste for Pepsi is a reflection of Pepsi's branding strategy.

I also own Mac. I used to try to convince PC people that Macs are better but have lately taken to a new (and more effective) strategy. When I'm asked why I use a Mac, I diffuse the issue by saying that, essentially, all personal computers (both Mac and PC) will do all the basic functions. And then I say, "It's kind of like this, 'Why do some people drive BMWs and some drive Fords? Both are cars; I just like BMWs.'" My PC friends are left wondering what it's like to "drive" a Mac. But the point is, I *own* the look, feel, image, logo, and name of Macintosh computers. I'm typing on a PowerBook G4. It's a year old and still turns heads every time I open it up. I'm convinced that Mac computers make me more productive. I have taken full ownership of the Mac brand.

Of course, to the Mac marketing team, Mac owns me. And I am a one-man Grassfire Effect for the Mac. I'm definitely one of the 20 percent who grow Mac's business. I'm branded.

GRASSFIRE EFFECTOR NO. 5—
CREATE CUSTOMER OWNERSHIP

The goal of branding is for your customers to think of your business or organization when they think of your core concept. When you think of civil liberties, does the ACLU come to mind? For animal rights maybe PETA comes to mind. For family issues, perhaps Focus on the Family.

At Grassfire.org, our core concept is bound up in our organization's name. We want to be the place where grassroots conservatives can start issue grassfires that impact the culture. At the end of the day, we hope conservative citizens associate online activism with Grassfire.org.

How can you brand yourself and create this ultimate ownership bridge to your customers and constituents? First, start thinking of your organization as a brand. Let your product or service be to you what Kleenex is to facial tissue. Be the first person to buy in to your own branding philosophy. Then draw a direct connection between your core concept and your brand in your communications.

For example, if you own Johnny's Restaurant that specializes in ribs, why not simply connect those dots and call it Johnny's Ribs? When your customers think ribs, over time they will begin to associate ribs with Johnny's.

Then, once "Johnny's" means "ribs," you could even go back and shorten your name to "Johnny's." I know I run the risk of wearing you out on Wal-Mart examples, but this is precisely what Sam Walton did. His first store was called Wal-Mart Discount City. Today, "Discount City" is unnecessary: Wal-Mart is the definition of discount retail.

How May We Serve You?

The greatest way to increase your Grassfire Effect can be summarized in one word: *service.* Jesus says, "The greatest among you will be your servant" (Matt. 23:11). It's part of what my friends and I call the Law of Inverse Propriety. At first glance, it just doesn't make sense that the greatest is the servant, but in the real world those who serve rule.

Consider any successful company and you will undoubtedly be able to boil down their business model to some core service. Even product-based companies serve by providing the product that best meets customers' needs. Every time I open a can of Pepsi, PepsiCo is meeting my need for affordable, accessible soft drinks. Pepsi is serving me.

GRASSFIRE EFFECTOR NO. 6— MEET BASIC NEEDS OF CUSTOMERS

Easy return policies and money-back guarantees are ways companies meet the basic need of worry-free shopping. In the Elliott home, there is a constant flow of purchases and returns. We are always sending something back. My friends will tell you that I'm the first to send back an entrée—even a cheeseburger—if it doesn't meet my satisfaction. Some companies don't even require you to keep your own receipt anymore—they will keep it all on file at the store for you. Just bring the item back. Please bring it back. Such companies understand the Grassfire Effect.

If you have traveled overseas, you know that American business is generally way ahead of other countries in meeting the need of worry-free shopping. In many countries, you are basically on your own. The life of the consumer is a constant battle with the stores. It's refreshing to come back to America where I can return almost any item within a reasonable time, no questions asked.

The question for you is, what are the basic needs of your customers or constituents? Have you asked your customers? Are you monitoring your complaints? People are generally satisfied if you will meet their basic needs, especially when you combine this with a friendly, small-town environment.

The Grassfire Meeting

Expanding your Grassfire Effect depends on your ability to create the right environment for the grassfire to burn brightly. And this environment hinges on meeting basic needs and building a bond with your customers.

As I said earlier, the Grassfire Effect should be a basic statistical measure of your business or organization. It also should be an integral part of your corporate culture. Every employee—top to bottom—should know and understand that your organization's success depends in large part on cultivating a stronger Grassfire Effect. If your team will buy in to the Grassfire Effect principle, a grassfire environment will naturally grow in your company.

How can you cultivate the idea of the Grassfire Effect in your organization? Try calling a Grassfire Meeting. It's a very short meeting designed to spawn ideas that will help your organization increase its Grassfire Effect by getting people to think in terms of the Grassfire Effect.

The Format: A Grassfire Meeting is no more than twenty-one minutes long. It starts precisely on time and ends precisely in twenty-one minutes, no questions asked.

The reason I suggest twenty-one minutes is because, in general, people don't like meetings. If you've lived in the corporate world, you know that meetings last too long and often seem to accomplish nothing. The other reason I like twenty-one minutes is that the total time for the entire meeting is no more than a half hour (including the minutes spent getting to the meeting and back to your desk). The twenty-one-minute format will be a shock at first because it will be over before your employees realize they are in a meeting. But they will leave feeling like they accomplished more in that meeting than most other meetings.

The Topic: Your Grassfire Meeting must be focused on one of two things: (1) meeting a basic need or (2) building a stronger bond.

The goal is to increase your organization's Grassfire Effect. Announce your Grassfire Meeting with an e-mail that sets out the parameters and states the goal and the topic. State that it is a twenty-one-minute brainstorming meeting to generate ideas. No one will believe you. Here's a sample e-mail.

Subject: Grassfire Meeting—Enhance drive-thru experience
To: Team@yourcompany.net
From: Steve Elliott
Date: Tuesday, September 7, 3:37 P.M.

Team,

We are holding a Grassfire Meeting tomorrow at 11 A.M. to brainstorm ways to enhance our drive-thru experience for our customers.

The meeting will last 21 minutes. Our goal will be to generate as many grassfire ideas as possible.

See you there!

Steve

The Meeting: Begin the meeting by stating its purpose: to increase your Grassfire Effect so that customers will grow your business. Then state the specific goal of the meeting. Perhaps you want to "grassfire" ideas on how to make the drive-thru experience better for your customers. Assign someone to take notes (a dry-erase board is handy). Then dive right into the content.

The Law of Twenty-One

What is the content of a Grassfire Meeting? In twenty-one minutes, your team will brainstorm twenty-one sparks of ideas that could possibly expand your Grassfire Effect. I call this the Law of Twenty-One—that on virtually any topic a small group of people can come up with twenty-one ideas in a matter of minutes. I've tried this out in different scenarios with all sorts of age groups and noticed a certain pattern in the process. First, the group is shocked by the daunting task of twenty-one brainstorms. It sounds impossible, especially in twenty-one minutes! In general, people have not trained their minds to think creatively. Also, most people worry that their idea isn't worthy of the group or that it will be scorned. So there is an initial pregnant pause. Then, finally, someone will pick off one of the obvious ideas. Slowly, one-by-one, the first six or seven ideas will emerge. But right at about idea number seven, the pace picks up. Suddenly, ideas start coming almost as fast as you can write them down. Often, the process slows again around fifteen or sixteen. Then it speeds up so that you will often find that you have to *stop* your team at twenty-one ideas.

Once you hit twenty-one ideas or twenty-one minutes, firmly and suddenly end your meeting. Announce that the Grassfire Meeting is over. Ask the meeting's secretary to distribute the twenty-one ideas by e-mail to each participant. Encourage everyone to review the twenty-one ideas, then plan a follow-up meeting to identify which ideas to pursue.

Creating a Grassfire Environment

The Grassfire Meeting can expand your organization's Grassfire Effect by creating for your employees the same grassfire-growing environment that you want your customers to experience. Think about the six Grassfire Effectors outlined in this chapter, as applied to your employees:

1. The *employee* is always Mom!
2. Learn your *employee's name.*
3. Make your *work environment* a "small town."
4. Cultivate *employee* opinion leaders.
5. Create *employee* ownership.
6. Meet the basic needs of *employees.*

The Grassfire Meeting is one way you can cultivate these values within your own organization. By making Grassfire Meetings accessible to all, you are saying the employees are "always Mom"— their ideas are valid. By having small-group Grassfire Meetings, you are working with your employees on a first-name basis and cultivating that small-town environment. Grassfire Meetings give your employee opinion leaders an opportunity to shine. As Grassfire Meeting ideas develop into reality in your organization, you will create an employee ownership bond that is stronger than their paychecks.

Finally, the Grassfire Meeting helps meet a basic need of your employees, which is beyond money (I'm assuming your employees receive market compensation). The basic need of human beings is for their lives to matter. At work, we all want what we do to make a difference, and we want our specific contribution to leave a mark. We want to matter. Remember, each person is *created* in the image of the Creator; your employees were born to be creative and make a difference in their world. In a practical way, eight hours a day, their world is your company. They were created to make a positive difference in your company. A simple twenty-one-minute investment can light a spark in your employees that could change your company and dramatically increase your Grassfire Effect.

At Grassfire.org, we live off the ideas of our staff. That's the advantage of having a small organization. No one person can possibly come up with all the good ideas. We constantly brainstorm ideas. We have a protocol for distributing concepts to the Grassfire team through what we call "IDEA" e-mails. We will try just about any new idea that two or three of us think is a good concept. Our bigger challenge is prioritizing which ideas to pursue. At the end of the year, when we look back at what we've accomplished, we can see the fingerprints of each of our employees all over everything we've done. We're always shocked that most of our best ideas were totally original in that year. And it reminds us that the next year's success will be birthed in fresh ideas.

In the next chapter, you'll discover a secret ingredient that will grow your Grassfire Effect in a dramatic way. This super-secret component will be like pouring gasoline on your grassfire. But first, take time right now to assess how you can apply these Grassfire Effectors to your relationship with your customers *and* your employees. And start growing your Grassfire Effect today!

KEY EFFECTS

1. Your customers control your Grassfire Effect.
2. The customer is always Mom!
3. Anonymity is the enemy of the Grassfire Effect.
4. Twenty percent of your customers drive 80 percent of your Grassfire Effect. Cultivate these 20 percent.

✔5. Customer and employee ownership will increase your Grassfire Effect.

✔6. Meeting basic needs should always be central to your focus.

✔7. The Grassfire Meeting can cultivate your Grassfire Effect.

FIRE STARTERS

🔥 On a scale of 1 to 10 (with 10 being the best), how is your organization doing with each of the Grassfire Effectors discussed in this chapter.

Grassfire Effector	*Your Rank*
The customer is always Mom!	_____
Learn your customer's name	_____
Make your business a "small town."	_____
Cultivate opinion leaders.	_____
Create customer ownership.	_____
Meet the basic needs of customers.	_____

🔥 Define the core need your business or organization meets, and identify three ways right now to improve your ability to meet that need.

Core need:

_____

_____

_____

_____

1.

2.

3.

🔥 What is your brand? _____

Do your customers "own" your brand at the basic level of communication? _____ yes   _____ no   _____not sure

🔥 On a scale of 1 to 10 (with 10 being the best) how is your organization doing with each of the Grassfire Effectors discussed in this chapter as related to *employees*.

Grassfire Effector	*Your Rank*
The employee is always Mom!	_____
Learn your employee's name.	_____
Make your work environment a "small town."	_____
Cultivate employee opinion leaders.	_____
Create employee ownership.	_____
Meet the basic needs of employees.	_____

🔥 Find a setting to try out a Grassfire Meeting. If you do not own a business or manage a staff, try a meeting in a more informal setting with friends or family members.

KEY INSIGHTS AHEAD:

- How Virginia Peanuts changed my world
- The central drama of life in one word
- What is the moral center of capitalism?
- How to tap into unlimited opportunities

Chapter 9

Gas for Your Grassfire

The Number One Ingredient for Growth

I've got something extremely valuable for you. In fact, once you have this in your personal portfolio, you will see your success begin to compound exponentially.

What I have for you has built more bridges than any construction firm. It has opened more doors than any doorman. It has paved more roads than those who built the interstate highway system. It has resolved more disputes than the most notable diplomat.

And it is the equivalent of pouring gas on your grassfire. What is it?

It's something I picked up from several people over many years. But at a key moment in the history of Grassfire, I put it into play.

Earlier, I shared how this amazing Grassfire team came together, gathered from Virginia to Iowa. About six months after our launch, Bob, Randy, and I were plowing ahead and starting to see real success. There was only one problem: the three of us had not yet settled our working relationship. How would Grassfire be organized? What role would each of us play? Where would we be based? What was our vision? There were a thousand unanswered questions. Now that this grassfire had been lit, we had to get a handle on it as quickly as possible or it could burn out of control and do more damage than good.

Oh yeah, there was one other thing: we had not yet met face-to-face.

Even though we had been working together on a daily basis, we had not yet shaken hands and looked each other in the eye. It was a big mistake—probably the single biggest mistake I made in this entire process. I should've gotten on a plane the minute I realized Grassfire was taking off.

Virtual offices are nice. Technology today allows us to work effectively without having all the players in the same room all the time. At Grassfire, we operate in four different offices now, but we are connected by e-mail, phones, FedEx, faxes, cell phones, and even Internet phones. But nothing can replace actually being in the same room together.

Six months into our launch, with all these questions hanging in the air and the very future of Grassfire in the balance, we simply had to meet. So I got on a plane and headed for the heartland.

But I didn't go empty-handed. I made sure to pack that "thing" I had picked up so many years ago—the most powerful door-opening, bridge-building, conflict-resolving force in the universe.

Picture the scene. I've landed in Des Moines and am headed for our rendezvous point, the Holiday Inn across the street from the airport. I had never even seen a picture of these two Iowa guys, so I didn't know them from Adam.

Those first moments were awkward for us because you really don't know how much you can trust someone until you have met him. But we each were excited and hopeful that the meeting would go well. It was as if we knew we were caught up in something that was bigger than us. We just had to get through these little details, such as, what do you look like? what's your wife's name? got kids?

We met that afternoon just to get acquainted and lay out the main issues. Then we went to the hotel's restaurant for dinner. That's when I pulled out this bridge-building, door-opening, conflict-resolving thing.

It was a bag of world-famous Virginia peanuts; a classic Dr. Seuss book, *One Fish, Two Fish, Red Fish, Blue Fish*; and a copy of my graduate thesis.

The Power of Peanuts

Those peanuts, a children's book, and an unheralded college thesis held the power to open doors and build bridges. Those items would prove to be pure gasoline poured on this thing we called Grassfire.

What is so special, you ask, about Virginia peanuts? If you have to ask, then you simply haven't savored Virginia's finest crop. But seriously, why would a Dr. Seuss book and a college thesis pack such a punch?

Because the most powerful bridge-building, door-opening, conflict-resolving force in the universe is nothing more than . . . a simple gift.

Giving exponentially increases your Grassfire Effect. Giving is like gasoline poured on the grassfire of your idea or your dream. Giving is the central drama of the entire universe and the focus of most human interactions.

Life as a Gift-Giving Drama

Am I overstating the case? Not a bit. Think of the stages of human life from birth to death. Gifts are everywhere. We give our children a name. Family and friends give us gifts. We greet each birthday with a gift, but why? Do we somehow merit something from others just because we have aged another 365 days, or are these gifts an instinctive response to the fact that we have been given the gift of another year of life?

Ever been part of a wedding party that didn't involve gifts? The maid of honor gives a bridal shower. The best man gives a bachelor party. The wife's family gives the wedding. The groom's family gives the rehearsal dinner. The bride and groom give gifts to the wedding party. Those who attend bring gifts that are often extravagant in cost or precious in personal sentiment. At the height of the ceremony, the couple exchanges the gifts of wedding rings, which remain on their hands as an enduring symbol of the gift of a life of commitment. Then, the wedding night comes and the highest point in the entire gift-giving drama takes place when the ultimate marital gift is given in a magical and intimate exchange. When this gift is being given for the first time, it is even more precious.

Gifts bond marriages. Gifts move mountains. Gifts build bridges. Gifts are like gasoline to your grassfire. Gifts are everywhere.

Did someone get a new job? Give him a gift. A new house? A gift. A raise? Let's celebrate. Christmas? A gift. Father's Day? Mother's Day? Birthdays? Retirement? A gift. You simply cannot escape the gift-giving drama that goes on all around us.

Giving and Commerce

Gift giving is at the heart of human commerce as well. Economic theorist George Gilder (mentioned earlier) has written extensively on the central role that giving plays in the market. Gilder establishes this premise with a review of what he calls "economic anthropology." Gilder dis-

cusses the anthropological roots of giving and economic
exchange, noting that gifts of an earlier era frequently
took the form of a feast. The feast would be given and
valuable gifts offered. The recipient would then return the
feast and offer gifts of greater value. As this process continued, the prosperity of the community grew.

In economic terms, Gilder calls the gift an "investment."
In his seminal work, *Wealth and Poverty*, here is how he
applies gift giving to capitalism:

> The unending offerings of entrepreneurs, investing
> capital, creating products, building businesses,
> inventing jobs, accumulating inventories—all long
> before any return is received, all without any assur-
> ance that the enterprise will not fail—constitute a
> pattern of giving that dwarfs . . . any primitive rite
> of exchange. Giving is the vital impulse and moral
> center of capitalism.[4]

Gilder points out that, too often, economists focus on
the "exchange mechanism" of the market—what type of
economy is in operation—instead of the true driving force
of the market, which is the gift. Gifts and giving (not the
market mechanisms) actually result in an increase in values and a growth in the economy.

For Gilder, viewing giving as the moral center of
capitalism requires a view of life based in faith. Those
who give understand that the world is governed from
above:

> Under capitalism, the ventures of reason are
> launched into a world ruled by morality and
> Providence. The gifts will succeed only to the
> extent that they are "altruistic" and spring from
> an understanding of the needs of others. They
> depend on faith in an essentially fair and respon-
> sive humanity. In such a world, one can give with-
> out a contract of compensation. One can venture

without the assurance of reward. One can seek the surprises of profit, rather than the more limited benefits of contractual pay. One can take initiatives amid radical perils and uncertainties.[5]

Gilder adds that this gift-giving process in capitalism is centered on finding and meeting the needs of others. And while gifts are given with an expectation of return, there is no guarantee of return. "Capitalism," says Gilder, "transforms the gift impulse into a disciplined process of creative investment based on a continuing analysis of the needs of others."[6]

Unlimited Opportunities

As we have discussed, having a strong Grassfire Effect means being focused on the needs of others. Giving accomplishes this objective—the well-given gift meets a need or touches a heart in an unforgettable way. But this is just the beginning of the gift's impact on the giver.

A gift-oriented perspective on life will focus you on the uncontrollable, exciting potential of great return. Instead of simply exchanging a bushel of corn for a set amount of dollars, why not *give* a bushel of corn? In a world ruled by faith, the gift of a bushel of corn has an unlimited potential return. That's why the stock market has a bigger potential return than a straight economic exchange. At a very basic level, you the investor are *giving* money to a company and trusting the company will increase the value of your gift. There is no guarantee that your gift will ever return even one dime—it is possible to lose your entire investment. It is also possible to reap a tenfold, hundredfold, or even thousandfold return on your investment "gift."

At Grassfire.org our focus is on giving citizens and partner organizations the tools and resources that expand their impact on issues. Our team tries every day to find ways to give to our online team as well as our partner organizations. We don't always give perfectly, but this is the core of our organization and the heart of our success. I am confident that, while Grassfire.org may change dramatically over the years, as long as we remain focused on giving, our Grassfire Effect will continue to grow.

Bill, my business mentor who taught me that the most vital component of every organization is its supporters, is always trying to find creative ways to give to his clients. He gives gifts, time, consultations, resources. He often even gives away his professional services. And he has continually given to me. For example, he not only gave me a real golf bag; he filled it with exotic clubs that I barely know how to use.

In fact, my entire professional journey into self-employment that ultimately led to Grassfire was sparked by a "gift" from Bill. I met him while I was interning in Washington, D.C., at Heritage Foundation, a conservative think tank. Bill liked my work and later referred me for my first freelance writing project. It was a job he simply could not do, so he gave me the referral, no strings attached. He could have asked for a referral fee, but he didn't. That freelance project opened my eyes to a world beyond the boundaries of employment and into entrepreneurialism.

Five years would pass before Bill and I would cross paths again and begin to work together on projects. One day when we were talking on the phone, reflecting on our first meeting and that freelance referral, I thanked him for what he had done. Then he reminded me of something I had done for him that I'd never registered as being very significant. After he gave me that referral, I sent him a Christmas gift—nothing special, usually some packaged dessert—and continued to send him a gift each year. Even though we were not in regular contact, those gifts told Bill that I had not forgotten what he had done. He said I was one of the few who ever came back to say thanks. Now, more than a decade after our first gift exchange, Bill and I keep looking for new opportunities to give, knowing that greater opportunities are always just ahead of us.

The Adventure of Giving

You see, every gift is an adventure without predetermined results, an open door to unknown opportunities, a bridge to some future destination, a spark to a world-changing grassfire. Yes, every gift is a risk. But life's rewards always come gift wrapped in risk.

There is power and liberty in a life-perspective of giving. If you are not a "giver," then you are going to be a "taker" or a "deserver." In other words, you will view your life as something that someone else owes you. The problem with that perspective is that *someone else* ultimately has power over you. You are depending on *someone else* doing something to satisfy your life. You are setting yourself up to be the victim.

Instead of viewing life as a victim, the giver can be forward-thinking. When you give, you exceed someone's expectations, and suddenly the balance of power in the relationship shifts to you. You now have the freedom to go the extra mile without it being a debt that you owe. Giving sets you free. Giving puts you on a plane of unlimited potential. Giving is the most proactive way to intentionally spread your personal Grassfire Effect.

Daily Gift Giving

Now apply this idea of gift giving to your daily life. What about your job? What if you viewed your career through the prism of gift giving? What hues would you see? What gifts can you give to your employer? How about the gift of a positive attitude? Could always showing up on time, even a few minutes early, be a gift worth giving? Could you give your employer some creative ideas that would improve the company? What if employers did the same? What if they were looking for ways to give to their employees to make their lives better and their jobs more productive? What if they gave bonuses and raises that actually rewarded and surprised their giving employees, while quickly encouraging those less productive to move on (instead of frustrating both employee and employer in a dead-end situation)?

Unfortunately, too many employer-employee relationships focus on what each party can *get* instead of what each party can give. The employer sees marginal productivity and increasing costs of salary and benefits. The employee sees lack of recognition and reward for a job well done. As a result, annual reviews end up being a confrontation between underappreciated employees and backed-into-a-corner employers.

If you focus on what you can *give* to your employers instead of what you will get from them, you will reap a tremendous return on your investment. Let's face it. You are going to work anyway. You might as well put on the giving grid and see what happens. It may not happen in this job, but it will eventually. Just keep giving.

Let's take a look at the spark of an idea you have been developing as you have read this book. Is there a gift at the center of your idea? How does your product or service fit into the gift-giving cycle? How can you give more?

How about at home? Are you a giver or a taker in your home? What if husbands and wives were constantly engaged in a surprising flow of gifts to one another? It would revolutionize any marriage. What if children and parents spent their energies looking for ways to give to each other? Of course, I'm not suggesting some fantasy world of perfect harmony. The nature of human relationships demands that there will be friction and tension. That said, a giving perspective on life is possible and achievable. In fact, it's right there for the taking as we start giving.

Give This Book Away!

Even the simplest gifts can have a powerful Grassfire Effect. Take this book, for example. Just by giving this book away, you will be able to see for yourself the power of the Grassfire Effect. Can you think of someone who could use a spark of inspiration? Give them your copy of *The Grassfire Effect*. Go ahead and try it! Ask them to read it and pass it on to a friend—filling out the special page at the front of this book.

Just for giving this book away, I want to send you a gift—a special bonus audio CD that includes additional materials on the Grassfire Effect. That's how convinced I am that this experiment in giving will pour gasoline on your Grassfire Effect as well as mine. Once you give a copy of this book to a friend, simply visit Grassfire Effect.com/bonusCD to receive your free CD.

The Ultimate Gift

Do you still doubt the power of the gift? Then I have some good news for you. Actually, I'm talking about the Good News—the central message of the world's largest religion. "For God loved the world in this way: He *gave* His One and Only Son, so that everyone who believes in Him will not perish but have eternal life" (John 3:16). Gift giving works for God. It will work for you.

Consider these two contemporary readings of
Luke 6:38:

"Give and men will give to you—yes, good
measure, pressed down, shaken together and running over will they pour into your lap. For whatever measure you use with other people, they will
use in their dealings with you." (Phillips)

"Give away your life; you'll find life given back,
but not merely given back—given back with

bonus and blessing. Giving, not getting, is the way. Generosity begets generosity." (*The Message*)

When I pulled out the homegrown Virginia's Finest Peanuts and the two books at the dinner table, I wasn't trying to position myself with Bob and Randy or get something from them. I was doing something out of who I am. This drama of giving had been instilled in my life through my experiences with family, friends, and most notably my wife, Stacy, the most sincere and generous person I know. Don't get me wrong. I don't always live this principle out perfectly. I'm stubborn and selfish quite often. But with these two guys from Iowa sitting across the dinner table from me, I simply wanted to give them something.

I'm not sure exactly what happened as those simple gifts were shared around that table at the Holiday Inn a few hours after we met, but I know the return I've received has been exponential. The next time we were together, Bob and Randy brought along gifts and the pattern of giving increased. Now, we can hardly get together without some gift being exchanged, but the point is, because our core team is giving-oriented, our corporate culture centers on giving.

Looking for some gas for your grassfire? Don't look too far. Just start giving.

Key Effects
1. Giving is the most powerful force in human relations and the fuel for your Grassfire Effect.
2. Giving is at the heart of capitalism.
3. Giving focuses you on the needs of others and offers an unlimited return.
4. A life perspective on giving is a choice you make.

FIRE STARTERS

🔥 There are two types of people in the world: givers and takers. What percentage of the time are you a giver or a taker?

_____% giver _____% taker

_____% not mindful of either

🔥 Economic interaction can be described as a series of gift exchanges. Describe the core concept of the idea you are developing or the product/service you are offering in terms of a gift. How is your core concept a gift?

_____

_____

_____

_____

_____

🔥 List ten ways you can give today in practical terms. Remember, gifts are usually not monetary and the size of the gift doesn't matter.

1.
2.
3.
4.
5.
6.
7.
8.
9.
10.

Put this principle of giving to the test by giving this book to a friend. Once you do, be sure to visit Grassfire Effect.com/bonusCD to receive my gift to you.

Chapter Notes

4. George Gilder, *Wealth and Poverty, A New Edition of the Classic* (San Francisco: Institute for Contemporary Studies, 1993), 27.

5. Ibid., 37.

6. Ibid., 31.

Chapter 10

Your Grassfire's History
Discovering the Power of Context

Each election year, the political parties work hard to register as many new voters as possible and then get those voters to the polls. At the end of the day, about six in ten Americans who are eligible actually vote. In 2004, a record turnout year, that translated into 122 million citizens voting and 78 million who were eligible not voting.

Still, voting is trumpeted as the fundamental right and responsibility of citizens. Voting is the most basic form of civic involvement that citizens should muster up. Voting is the foundation of our rights as citizens.

Or is it?

What if I told you there was a civic action that predates voting and can be argued as being more influential than voting in shaping the course of British and American civil society?

What if I told you there is a deeper well for citizen activism than voting that every citizen has the *right* to tap into anytime he wants?

Would you believe me?

Would you be interested in finding out what that right is?

I'll let you in on this little secret right to demonstrate a vital principle that you must grasp to truly tap in to your own Grassfire Effect. This principle will come into focus as we connect the dots between this age-old right, Grassfire.org, and your personal grassfire.

As the old proverb says, "There is nothing new under the sun." Yes, you will have sparks of imagination and creativity and inspiration. But everything you do happens in a broader context—a historical context that can add a deeper meaning and purpose to your life. To begin connecting these dots, let's explore the driving force behind Grassfire.org and how this relates to this secret right.

Wanting to Have an Impact

For me, Grassfire.org has always been driven by two words: *real impact.* Growing up in New England, it seemed the world operated on rules set in place three hundred years ago, which left no room for me to impact that world. Even after we had lived in our little town in Connecticut for a decade, to the "old salts" we were still the new kids on the block.

During my teenage years, my worldview began to change. I became a Christian and as a result discovered a new world. I learned that "this is my Father's world" and I had a place in that world. I went to college and then graduate school where I studied public policy and learned the inner workings of the government. I wanted to have a real impact on my world, and this desire followed me to Grassfire.org.

Today, behind everything we do at Grassfire is that same desire for impact—to turn the lone voices of grassroots Americans into a united chorus that can make a difference on key issues.

When we supported the Boy Scouts, we discovered the real impact we could have, rallying citizens to take action at a moment's notice. We saw impact, at both regional and national levels. We saw legislation passed to secure the Scouts' right to equal access to public facilities.

Shutting Down Senator Daschle's Office

Time and again, we have repeated this Grassfire strategy. In the summer prior to the 2002 elections, we launched a campaign to urge then-majority leader Senator Tom Daschle to take action on more than fifty bills that had passed the House and were awaiting action in the Senate. It was a clear case of political obstructionism in our opinion. Daschle simply was not going to move on a host of bills, including a ban on partial-birth abortion that he had voted in favor of on three prior occasions.

Tens of thousands of citizens joined with us, and we arranged a petition delivery to Daschle's office. Just one problem: Daschle's office refused to accept the petitions. Twice. For the record, his office stated that new 9/11 security protocols prohibited their office from accepting hand-delivered petitions. However, our team had on many occasions delivered petitions to other Senate leaders in Daschle's office building after 9/11. In our opinion, the majority leader simply did not want to feel the heat from our Grassfire team.

Bad idea. It would have been better for Daschle's team to simply accept our petitions because those boxes of petitions truly represented citizens from across the country who felt strongly about this issue. We weren't blowing smoke. We had a real grassfire on our hands.

We let our team know that Daschle had refused to accept our petitions, and the senator's switchboard started lighting up. For days, his team scrambled to handle the flood of calls from Grassfire team members. Following his office's instructions to us, we made a third attempt at a delivery and arrived with a Capitol Hill postal courier in tow and this time succeeded. When we arrived, two aides were busy answering phones. When we identified ourselves, one of the aides said, "I just got off the phone with a Grassfire person." At first, Daschle's staffers didn't want to accept the petitions but finally relented. We even managed to snap a photo and place it on our Web site. Just weeks later, Daschle's team responded personally to many of our supporters on this issue. One of our team members from his home state of South Dakota let us know just how appreciative she was of our effort.

She wrote us to say that Daschle had personally written her, urging her not to sign Grassfire petitions, and that if she wanted to talk to him, all she had to do was call. She didn't believe him because she'd been getting our updates and had been making many phone calls to the senator — never with a personal response.

Instead, she started her own grassfire right in South Dakota — one designed to oust the senator when his term was up. Did she make a difference? Well, just ask *former* Senate minority leader Daschle, who in November 2004 became the first party leader in the Senate to be defeated for reelection in more than a half century.

By the way, a few months after Grassfire's encounter with then-Senator Daschle, we found out just how impactful that effort had been. During another visit to our congressional leaders on Capitol Hill, Ron — a key member of our Grassfire.org communications team — introduced himself to a Hill staffer and mentioned that he was with Grassfire.

The staffer replied, "I know you guys. You're the ones who shut down Senator Daschle's office!"

Ron was a bit surprised. "How did you hear about that?" he asked.

"It was the talk of the third floor of the Senate office building," the Hill staffer added. "You shut down their phones and faxes! It was awesome."

It was only then that Ron realized the full impact of our Grassfire team. But there's more. Ron then met with a key U.S. senator and introduced himself. The senator smiled and replied, "I know who you are. You're the ones who shut down Senator Daschle's office!" A small spark had lit a fire on Capitol Hill.

Saving the Pledge

Perhaps the most significant issue we tackled in those first few years involved the Pledge of Allegiance. In July 2002, a three-judge panel of the Ninth Circuit Court of Appeals issued a ruling that found the words "under God" in the Pledge of Allegiance unconstitutional. The ruling would mean that children in nine states would not be allowed to say the words "under God" as part of the recitation of the Pledge, further establishing in our jurisprudence a blatant hostility toward any public acknowledgment of God.

Within minutes of the ruling, we were receiving e-mails from Grassfire team members urging us to take action. Before nightfall, we had launched a petition to save the Pledge. By morning, more than four thousand people were signing the petition every hour, and the signers kept coming for days.

Over the next months, we rallied more than half a million citizens on the Pledge issue. Just as important, we gave these citizens action points to make a difference in this case. First, we flooded the Ninth Circuit with phone

calls, letters, and faxes. Next, we filed an *amicus brief* to the
court (an *amicus brief* is a "friend of the court" brief that citizens can file as an official part of the case). Instead of filing as an individual or generically as an organization, we
set up an online "signing" form and asked our team members to co-sign our brief, eventually garnering more than
forty-five thousand cosigners! Interestingly, that strategy
came as a result of a spark of an idea one of our staff members had after talking with a clerk at the Ninth Circuit. We
knew organizations often filed such briefs in cases, but we
had never heard of a group mobilizing actual *cosigners* to a
brief.

We continued to follow this case for months as it
slowly progressed to the United States Supreme Court. At
that point, we heard from many of our team members as
well as the media that grassroots pressure would be mean-
ingless. The Supreme Court was simply beyond the reach
of the grassroots citizen. Citizens could do nothing to
influence the federal courts and certainly not the Supreme
Court.

We at Grassfire had a different theory. Our presump-
tion was that the members of the Supreme Court were
ultimately servants of the citizens of the United States.
Supreme Court justices derive their authority from the
Constitution, which derives its authority from the people.
Also, the Constitution specifically declares that Supreme
Court justices "shall hold their offices during *good behav-
iour.*" In my mind, that is an important qualifier that places
the Court in a position of accountability to the people.

Those justices are human beings like you and me. They
consider cases and issue rulings in the context of the culture in which they live. We had seen the Ninth Circuit
take a very measured approach after the grassroots
response to its initial ruling. We wanted to make sure
those nine Supreme Court justices understood that citi-

zens across the nation would be monitoring this case very closely every step of the way.

The first step was to encourage the Court to accept the case. So we rallied citizens to send tens of thousands of personal letters to the Supreme Court. The Supreme Court accepted the case, and we moved to the next phase of our campaign to save the Pledge. Working with the Common Good Legal Foundation, we developed an official amicus brief to be submitted to the Supreme Court. Once again, we asked our team members to consider cosigning our brief and becoming an official part of this historic case. In all, more than 174,000 citizens cosigned Grassfire's amicus brief on this case.

To put that in perspective, in February of 2003 (less than a year prior to our brief filing), a group of law students from 139 law schools teamed together to file an amicus brief before the Supreme Court. Their news release claimed: "The brief likely represents the largest group of individuals to ever join together to file an amicus brief in the history of the Supreme Court." Their cosigners totaled thirteen thousand people. A few months later, a little grassfire had spread to eclipse that prior cosigner record by 1,200 percent.

Our brief afforded me the opportunity to sit in the chambers as the Court heard the oral arguments in the case of *Newdow v. Congress* that would decide the fate of the Pledge and would affect all citizens' right to publicly acknowledge God. Thankfully, the Supreme Court overturned the lower court ruling, preserving the right of students to say the Pledge with the words "under God."

I am convinced that grassroots pressure saved the Pledge and influenced how the Supreme Court handled this case. It was clear from the wording of the Court's majority opinion that the justices lacked the will to go on record affirming the constitutionality of "under God" in the Pledge. I suspect that Chief Justice William Rehnquist—nearing the end of his term—wanted to issue a strong ruling on the subject and establish clear jurisprudence on the public acknowledgment of God. Chief Justice Rehnquist wrote a concurring opinion that expressly affirmed the constitutionality of "under God" in the Pledge. But for his opinion to become the majority opinion in the case, he would need four other justices to join with him. Only two other justices co-signed Rehnquist's opinion. Instead, the majority opinion was, in effect, a ruling on a technicality that did not support the constitutional right to acknowledge God. In my opinion, the liberals on the Supreme Court did not want to establish clear jurisprudence on the right to acknowledge God, but they could not go so far as to uphold the lower court ruling that banned the words "under God" from the Pledge. That's because this case was being decided less than six months prior to a presidential election on an issue that was clearly a political lightning rod for conservatives. A ruling by the Court *against* the Pledge would have set off an unprecedented grassroots backlash that would likely have had repercussions that extended to the presidential election later that year. Grassroots pressure constrained a liberal court that, left to its own devices, may well have stricken "under God" from the Pledge.

On June 14, 2004, the Court issued its ruling in the Pledge case. If you could have visited the Supreme Court in Washington, D.C., on that day, you might have noticed a large banner on display immediately across the street from the entrance to the justices' private parking garage on the east side of the Supreme Court building, proclaiming "50 Years Under God." Earlier that month, Grassfire.org and our partners at the National Clergy Council erected the banner to commemorate the fiftieth anniversary of the addition of "under God" in the Pledge.

I can't say for sure that the justices saw our banner that day as they came to the Supreme Court. I can't confirm that the justices read the thousands of letters from Grassfire team members or acknowledged our petition delivery of six hundred thousand petitions or specifically referenced our amicus brief. But it is interesting that the justices would issue their ruling in the Pledge case on June 14, 2004, because that was precisely the fiftieth anniversary our banner was commemorating. I'm sure the justices would say this was all just a coincidence.

In the Center of the Marriage Debate

Another example of the impact Grassfire has had involves the marriage advocacy movement in our nation. Before this issue made national headlines, Grassfire was working to rally citizens to support the Marriage Protection Amendment. We began this effort when there was little momentum for the amendment.

About fifteen months after we had begun, our petitions were being personally presented to the Senate majority leader and then were delivered by Senate staffers to each Senate office (thanks to the alliances and partnerships we were developing). You see, issues advocacy is an intensely competitive environment. Organizations compete with each other to take credit for successes, identify supporters, and expand their influence. Our philosophy has been quite different. Perhaps to a fault, Grassfire has taken the back seat in many efforts involving other organizations. But these partnerships have greatly enhanced our impact on the issues. Such was the case with the marriage issue.

Even though we lost that first Senate vote, the event was anything but a defeat. We heard reports that senators were recording all-time highs in constituency phone calls, faxes, and e-mails. No other issue had resulted in such a strong grassroots response in many senators' entire tenure in the Senate. And because we had a long-term strategy, we clearly established from the beginning that our goal was to build momentum at each opportunity and continue working until passage was secured.

This is precisely what has happened since that first Senate vote. Grassfire and other organizations have continued to build grassroots support. This support has grown with each new court case determining a homosexual right to marry. As I write, it is clear that the federal courts are determined to create by fiat a full constitutional right for homosexuals to marry. Given what has already happened in the state courts, the federal courts, and the Supreme Court, this is almost an inevitability. In fact, homosexual activists are rushing to push their agenda through the courts, hoping to move faster than the Marriage Protection Amendment can progress.

We will win this debate for two reasons. First, I am convinced that grassroots momentum is clearly on the side of securing marriage as the union of one man and one woman. Second, we are also on the side of history.

The framers of the Constitution set up a process whereby laws are passed and rights are secured. This process is outlined in the Constitution. The social planners have been using the courts to reshape society, but that was never the process set out by the Constitution. All legislative power—lawmaking power—has been vested in the Congress not the courts. And there is a specific process outlined for amending the Constitution, a process we are following and will continue to follow until we see victory.

In Step with History

These are only a few examples of how Grassfire is having an impact on the key issues of our day. But to explain what this entire discussion of Grassfire's impact has to do with *your* Grassfire Effect, let's step back in time to when kings ruled the British empire and subjects had little recourse. As far back as 1215, King John's charter referenced a process of subjects appealing to lower magistrates, and in turn the magistrates would lay before the king the transgression, asking that the transgression "be corrected without delay." For hundreds of years, it was understood that British subjects enjoyed this right of laying before the king their issues of concern—that is, petitioning their government.

In 1689, this right to petition was codified in the English Bill of Rights. The fifth clause of the rights of the people states, "That it is the right of the subjects to petition the King, and all commitments and prosecutions for such petitioning are illegal."

The listing of this right in the Bill of Rights was an outgrowth of the Seven Bishops Case in 1688 in which a group of bishops petitioned the king, resisting his order to have his Declaration of Indulgence read in their churches. Despite the king's efforts to stack the court against the bishops, the bishops were found not guilty.

Across the pond in America, the British subjects living in the colonies understood this right to petition the king and often invoked this right in their documents. The resolutions of the Stamp Act Congress in 1765 affirmed "that it is the right of the British subjects in these colonies, to petition the king or either house of parliament." By 1774, the Resolves of the First Continental Congress was more explicit: "That they have a right peaceably to assemble, consider of their grievances, and petition the king; and that all prosecutions, prohibitory proclamations, and commitments for the same, are illegal."

In the minds of the colonists, this right to petition was being trampled upon by the king. Just two years later, the colonists set out finally to break from Britain. In their minds, it was their final option. Their Declaration of

Independence listed a "long train of abuses and usurpations" that was evidence of "a design to reduce them under absolute despotism." But it was not simply the abuses of the king that were the final straw. After listing the abuses, they said: "In every stage of these oppressions we have petitioned for redress in the most humble terms. Our repeated petitions have been answered only by repeated injury."

If this right of petition had been honored by the king and parliament, it is doubtful the colonists would have taken up arms.

Petitions in America

The history of petitions did not end with the Declaration of Independence. When it came time to draft the Bill of Rights, this right to petition was prominently positioned as part of the First Amendment: "Congress shall make no law respecting an establishment of religion, or prohibiting the free exercise thereof; or abridging the freedom of speech, or of the press; or the right of the people peaceably to assemble, and to *petition the government for a redress of grievances*" (emphasis added).

The right to petition the government was so essential that it was included alongside the free exercise of religion, speech, the press, and the right to assemble. America's founders understood their heritage of British rights. Instead of being subjects of the king, they were now people with certain rights. Let's not forget that these rights enumerated in the Bill of Rights were considered so fundamental that many at that time opposed the idea of actually enumerating some rights for fear that other rights would be excluded (thus, the Ninth and Tenth Amendments).

It gets better: Petitioning is a more fundamental right than even *voting!* At the time of the First Amendment, women, free blacks, and slaves could not vote. But they could petition. According to the Library of Congress, "in Virginia, the right to petition was not restricted by any requirements involving class, sex, or even race. Members of all social classes exercised their right to petition and received responsive action from their government. Although they were denied the right to vote, women, free blacks, and occasionally even slaves employed petitions to participate in the political process and make their opinions known."

The right to petition *preceded* and *superceded* even the right to vote. The right to petition gave even those who could not vote the potential to have their grievances heard by the government. Virginia has a strong heritage of petitioning. In the seventeenth century, most legislation that passed in Virginia originated from petitions. Some of the most notable documents in American history were, in fact, petitions. James Madison's "Memorial and Remonstrance" is perhaps the most famous of all petitions. The historic "Ten-Thousand Name" petition launched the debate over the role of church and state that culminated in the Virginia Declaration of Religious Liberties.

This pattern of petitioning continued in Virginia well into the nineteenth century. The Library of Virginia contains a collection of twenty thousand petitions from 1776 to 1865, demonstrating the importance of petitions in early American history. Petitions were common practice throughout the states and in Congress during this founding time in our nation.

Slavery Petitions

One of the most important political debates in American history—the question of slavery—was a forum for countless petitions being presented to local, state, and federal legislatures for consideration. John Quincy Adams led the abolition effort in the House of Representatives, fighting continuously to have the issue of slavery heard on the floor of the House. In 1834, the American Anti-Slavery Society launched a nationwide petition drive. Petitions began to flood Congress by the hundreds and then thousands. Per House rules, each petition had to be heard on the floor and entered into the record. The proslavery contingent decided to put an end to the petitions and on May 25, 1836, passed the "gag rule," which caused all slavery petitions to be automatically tabled without being heard on the floor of the House or being entered into the record. Here is the resolution, which passed 117 to 68: "Resolved, that all petitions, memorials, resolutions, propositions, or papers, relating in any way or to any extent whatever to the subject of slavery, or the abolition of slavery, shall, without being either printed or referred, be laid upon the table, and that no further action whatever shall be had thereon."

In response to the resolution, Adams said, "Am I gagged, or am I not?"—thus, the name gag rule. The rule only increased the flow of antislavery petitions to a flood. The House Journal of January 30, 1837, reports that Adams himself submitted twenty-three petitions to abolish slavery in the District of Columbia that day. Also on January 30, other members of the House submitted at least forty-nine additional petitions. In all, from 1837 to 1838 an astounding 130,000 antislavery petitions were submitted to Congress. It took Adams and the abolitionists eight years to have the gag rule rescinded, restoring the First Amendment right to petition the government on this issue. On December 3, 1844, the rule was rescinded by a vote of 108 to 80. That evening, Adams recorded these words in his diary: "Blessed, forever Blessed, be the name of God!"

The antislavery gag rule and the flood of petitions that followed during the eight long years of debate regarding this issue helped to galvanize abolitionist support. It was an important part of a grassroots effort that would eventually force the divided nation to confront the evil of slavery.

But again, what does this all have to do with *your* grassfire? Let's begin connecting the dots.

When the spark of an idea for Grassfire.org began in my mind and in the hearts of a few close friends, we quickly realized that we could be a part of something that could have a real impact on our nation. But we had no idea that what we were doing had such deep roots in American history. I was not thinking about the fact that the central premise of Grassfire—petitioning our leaders—was enshrined as a right in the First Amendment. Every day, Grassfire uses the tools of the Internet to rally citizens to sign petitions and take an active stand on issues. If he were alive today, John Quincy Adams would be using the Internet in a similar manner to what we are doing at Grassfire to rally citizen petitions.

What we are doing is not just a nice thing; it's much more. The right to petition is fundamental to the experience of western civilization. It was vital in the establishment of the colonies. Petitions were instrumental in the decision to declare independence. Petitions inspired most legislation that was written for much of our nation's early history. Petitions played a central role in the most important debate in American history—slavery.

Again, there is "nothing new under the sun." But that's not a bad thing. In fact, discovering the historical context of petitions injects meaning and purpose into everything we do at Grassfire. We are walking in the footprints of Thomas Jefferson, Benjamin Franklin, and John Adams. The historical context also extends the timeline for what we are doing. No longer are we rallying citizens on a specific issue at one point in time. We are upholding this right to petition, which was secured generations ago, for generations to come. Our timeline extends from 1200 to 2200.

Petitioning also has a very personal historical context for me. My mom, our family historian, has shared stories of our family's civic heritage, especially that of her father. Ernest Segre-Lewis was willing to speak boldly before the governing authorities in his native land of Jamaica. He understood his right to petition. Two generations later, his legacy of civic involvement lives on in his grandson and is already clearly evident in the generation that follows me.

Your Grassfire's History

Now let's connect the dots to *your* life. There is a historical context for your personal grassfire — that idea that is stirring in your mind and heart. Someone before you, in some way, has carried the torch that is now coming to you. This someone developed some aspect of that idea and paved a way for you to ignite a grassfire in your world.

Your historical context may take some work to discover. You may find it in an old, dusty book in a library. You may find it in stories of family members who are now long gone. But if you will search, you will find the context. This context will help infuse what you do with meaning, purpose, and satisfaction. Just as important, you will discover that this torch — this grassfire — that you now have has been given to you as a trust to carry forward for future generations.

Finding Satisfaction in Life

Webster's defines satisfaction as the state of having one's needs or desires fulfilled. At the very core of your idea, there must be something that you want to accomplish that will bring you fulfillment and satisfaction.

Unfortunately, for too many people, the Rolling Stones got it right: *I can't get no satisfaction.*

For too many, life offers little fulfillment. But I believe the primary cause for an unsatisfied life is the lack of historical context. That is why even financial wealth will not satisfy if that wealth has no context—no connection to those who have gone before and those who will follow.

At Grassfire.org we have seen enough positive results to know that we are having an impact, which gives me satisfaction. I would say that there are few organizations that can light up the Capitol Hill switchboard as fast or as effectively as Grassfire.org. And every day, our team has the satisfaction of receiving e-mails from Grassfire friends who have caught the vision and are excited about having a real impact on issues.

Even on the most discouraging days, I can draw on the historical context and find meaning and purpose in what we are doing. It's as if John Adams has passed the torch to Grassfire!

How about you? Are you struggling to find meaning and satisfaction in what you have set your hands to do? Maybe your job feels like a dead end. Then try this: take a few minutes on the Internet and research the history of what your company does. Suppose you are a trash collector. With minimal effort, you can discover books on the social history of trash, reports on the history of garbage collection, and accounts of what has happened to cities (like New York) during garbage-collector strikes. You'll conclude that civilization simply cannot survive without garbage collection. If you will allow it, a historical context can transform the drudgery of your daily tasks into something full of meaning.

It is no accident that on the walls of many Chick-Fil-A restaurants is the story of founder Truett Cathy and how the chicken sandwich was invented. There's the picture of that first little restaurant; there's a mark on the timeline of when Cathy "invented" the chicken sandwich; there's the moment in time when Chick-Fil-A got a foothold in the malls and pioneered the food court; there's a reference to the Sundays-off policy; and there's the discussion of Chick-Fil-A's philanthropic efforts to help the community. Those messages speak volumes to both employees and customers and put that chicken sandwich in a historical context that has meaning and purpose. If you want your family, business, church, club, school, community, political campaign, or bowling league to succeed, historical context must be communicated. It is a central component to what communication theorists call a "rhetorical vision." Any business or gathering of people that lacks or forgets its historical context will either die out or stray so far from its purpose that it will become impotent and ineffectual.

All the great vision casters have understood the power of the historical context. Think of the best communicators in history: Winston Churchill, Ronald Reagan, Franklin Roosevelt, Martin Luther King. Each of these great communicators placed the issues of their times in a historical context. Perhaps the greatest address in American history, the Gettysburg Address, was all about creating a historical context that reached back to the Declaration of Independence ("Fourscore and seven years ago") and extended to the future destiny of America (that the "government of the people, by the people, for the people, shall not perish from the earth"). Lincoln's context of past and future empowered our nation to endure the terrible tragedy of the Civil War and continues to guide our nation nearly 150 years later.

Find Your Historical Context

If your whole life seems to lack meaning, then take hold of your own historical context. Begin to see your life not just as this moment in time; envision the historical context of your life. Think about family members who have gone before you and paid a high price so you could have the opportunities you have. Even if you come from the worst imaginable history, if you will open your mind and heart to this idea of finding a context for your life, you will see that there have been people somewhere in your past who paved the way for you. Ultimately, faith can provide that historical context. For example, the entire Christian religion is based on this concept of historical context: Christ died for me in the past so that I can experience freedom in the present and have hope for the future.

Even if you struggle to find a historical context in the past, you can always find one in your future. It may be your children, grandchildren, and even great-grandchildren. Those who are yet to be born are relying on you to take hold of this historical context for your life. You may never have children, but you will be part of someone else's historical context. Even the most menial tasks that you do today have generational impact. That's the Grassfire Effect, multiplied and amplified by an understanding of the historical context of your life.

Don't be distracted by Madison Avenue's or Hollywood's visions of satisfaction or meaning or purpose. Our marketing culture tries to focus us on the surface things. The real fuel for your grassfire will come from that well deep within you—from tapping into that historical context in the past and the future that will infuse your today with meaning. When you tap into the power of historical context, you'll find enough satisfaction to fuel a grassfire that extends across generations!

KEY EFFECTS

✎1. Life was meant to be satisfying and fulfilling.

✎2. John Quincy Adams passed the torch to Grassfire .org.

✎3. Historical context will infuse your life and ideas with meaning and purpose.

⚆ 4. Historical context reaches into the past and extends into the future.

⚆ 5. Every person and every organization has a historical context. Understanding and communicating that context will greatly increase your Grassfire Effect.

FIRE STARTERS

🔥 Jot down the names of a few individuals who help make up your historical context. Think of family members and others who have helped to pave the way for you.

_____

_____

🔥 What is the historical context for your current job? Write it out in a few sentences.

_____

_____

🔥 Can you state the historical context of the grassfire idea you are developing? Be bold and put your idea in historical context—drawing on those who went before you as well as your own rags-to-riches story (even if you only have the rags part thus far). Below or on a sheet of paper, write the historical context for your idea. Keep it short, no more than two paragraphs.

_____

_____

_____

_____

_____

_____

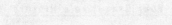

Conclusion
Taking the Next Step

KEY INSIGHTS AHEAD:

- *How to apply the principles of this book*
- *Are you a pipe-dreamer?*
- *Three levels of application for your Grassfire Effect*
- *Developing your life as a grassfire*

Chapter 11

Where Is Your Grassfire?

Charting Your Progress

We began this journey with the *idea* that the world is changed through ideas and with the belief that each person was created to have such ideas and to turn these ideas into world-changing reality.

I'll admit that this is an optimistic view of life. I believe in the untapped potential in every human being. And I am confident that one small spark can change your world. Again, the goal here is to change *your* world not the entire world. If each of us will focus on grassfires that change our own worlds, the entire world will be changed.

I hope that section 1 of this book inspired you to rekindle those sparks of ideas that may have been lying dormant in your mind and heart for years. Understand where these ideas come from and how you can begin cultivating an increasing flow of sparks of ideas in your daily life. By now you have grasped the essential truth that life is about people and that your grassfire idea must also be about people. Perhaps you have even found a core group of friends to help you develop your spark of an idea, and maybe you have already set a goal that will demand your respect and your hard work until it becomes reality. I also trust that you now are seeing success and failure as bumps along the same road that leads to turning your dreams into world-changing reality.

With this foundation of how grassfires are ignited, I trust section 2 has provided you with a new matrix for looking at how simple ideas develop world-changing momentum. The Grassfire Effect is the *inevitable result of your expanding circle of influence*. It is a principle that describes why and how some organizations grow exponentially and others seem to stagnate. It is the fundamental principle of growth for any organization and should be tracked. The Grassfire Effect is also an economic philosophy based on the unlimited potential of human life.

Even more important, the Grassfire Effect is a grid or a worldview for a prosperous and fulfilled life. As you come to the book's conclusion, I hope you can envision that first spark igniting in a field, dancing on a single blade of grass until a gust of wind comes and carries it to another blade. Then those two blades catch fire and cause the flame to spread to another, then another, then another until that one spark is now heading across the field. That fast-spreading grassfire has an exciting and unlimited potential impact on its world. And that spark is *you!*

A Warning to the Pipe-Dreamers

At the close of each chapter, I included principles and exercises to help you apply the concepts of the Grassfire Effect to your life. The one danger of this kind of motivational book is if it creates initial excitement and enthusiasm that does not translate into lasting change. The spark is ignited, bursts into flame, and then dies out.

In fact, there is a danger that so-called pipe-dreamers will use this book as an excuse to never get anything done. We all know the types. The phrase *pipe dream* was coined in the nineteenth century to describe the kind of flight of fancy induced by the smoking of an opium pipe. It's a fanciful dream produced by an altered or unrealistic state of mind, a dream birthed in nonreality. Pipe-dreamers live either vicariously through other people's dreams or flitter from one unrealistic million-dollar idea to the next without building real momentum in their lives. Please note that this book was never intended to encourage the pipe-dreamer to continue to chase or cultivate fantasies. If you are a pipe-dreamer, let me challenge you to step out of that fantasy world and apply the principles of the Grassfire Effect to your everyday world, like your job and your family. Don't use this book to further torment your loved ones with your unwillingness to serve and work in real ways that build steady momentum in your life.

How to Apply This Book

Most of us are not unrealistic dreamers. We are the opposite—hard-working, good-hearted folk who have great ideas but are not sure how to turn those ideas into reality. We have the potential for a Grassfire Effect that can change our world. Again, the challenge of this book comes down to practical application.

From the outset, I have envisioned three basic areas of application for the principles of the Grassfire Effect. First, let me challenge you to apply these principles to your current employment. The fact is, most of us spend the majority of our waking hours doing some type of work (or schooling). This is where we can find the most practical application for the principles of the Grassfire Effect.

For the dreamer, there is accountability in the daily chore. Instead of taking this book and creating another pipe dream, build grassfire momentum right in your job. As you allow these principles to transform how you look at your daily work, you will begin building a Grassfire Effect that will set you free from pipe dreaming and give those close to you hope that you can break the destructive cycle of illusion. So put your hand to the plow.

If you're not a pipe-dreamer, your job is still the best and most important place to begin applying the principles of this book. Let the ideas I've shared transform how you view your work. Turn your nine-to-five job from mundane to magnificent! It really isn't that hard. Take hold of the historical context of what your company does and what you do specifically within your company. Set out to serve the needs of those around you. And begin cultivating sparks of ideas that can change your job, make you more productive, and ultimately cause your boss and your company to succeed.

That daily duty called a job will always be there, no matter how successful you become. You will always have to put on your pants and do something called work. And that work will always be the best proving ground for your Grassfire Effect. So start there, with your current job, and apply these world-changing principles.

Cultivating Your Idea

The second area of application for this book is the realm of *new* ideas and *new* ventures and *new* opportunities. While you are cultivating your Grassfire Effect in your current job (remember, that comes first!), you can also begin cultivating those sparks of ideas that can transform your world.

In taking your idea from spark to reality, this book can serve as a blueprint. Section 1 will help you cultivate and develop your idea, taking it from your mind to your world. Section 2 will help you apply the principles of the

Grassfire Effect to maximize your growth and impact. Be mindful that there is no timeline. You could be developing your idea for months or even years before you move to the reality phase. That is why it is crucial to develop a close circle of friends who can walk this road with you and keep you moving steadily forward.

In fact, I strongly recommend that you work through this book with a friend. Go chapter-by-chapter and discuss the Grassfire Effects in each section. Talk through the challenges of your current job or the idea you are developing with your friend. And do the same for your friend — challenge him to apply these principles to his current job and to that latent spark of an idea that needs to be fanned into flame.

When you have finished this book, give it away or buy a copy for a friend and watch what this simple act of giving can do. You just may start a grassfire in your friend's life and expand your own Grassfire Effect! (And remember to visit GrassfireEffect.com/bonusCD so I can send you a bonus CD as my gift to you.)

Your Life as a Grassfire

The third area of application for this book is at the worldview level. I hope you will take the idea of grassfire and incorporate it into how you view your world. Again, your life is that spark. View your entire life in a historical context. See that you are running a race and others have passed the baton to you, and you will pass the baton to another generation. The influence of your life can reach countless thousands and even millions of people if you will be faithful today to cultivate your personal Grassfire Effect. But it doesn't take great global concepts to change your world. Most often, it is the simplest act of service and giving that has the greatest impact — something as simple as giving this book to a friend could start a grassfire in your friend's life that could have world-changing implications.

I see my life as a grassfire and hope you do as well. I truly believe that what I am doing today will impact many people, most notably my wife and our children. Every day, I am passing the torch in a small way to Anna, Hope, Kirsten, Lauren, and Samuel. But more than that, my life today is impacting and influencing their children's children and generations thereafter. That's far beyond the horizon of my seventy or eighty years. That's a context that can infuse my every day with meaning and purpose. That's a spark that can become a world-changing grassfire!

There's just one more story to tell. . . .

Chapter 12
A Harlot's Grassfire

Once upon a time . . .

That's usually how fairy tales and legends start. But this story is anything but a fairy tale. It's very much real life, one of the most dramatic and unexpected encounters in human history.

It's a story of a grassfire that was sparked two thousand years ago through one woman's life, changing the way people view their world. It demonstrates the power of the Grassfire Effect and emphasizes the point that grassfires can get started at the most improbable times, in the most unusual places, for the most unexpected reasons, and through the most unlikely people.

Even a harlot.

Or so our imagination would lead us to believe.

She lived in a village on the outskirts of the main city with the other half breeds of her community. These half breeds were considered outcasts by those in the city. Their lineage wasn't from the pure stock. Their customs were deemed a mockery. Those from the big city were not even supposed to pass through this half-breed village.

Then there was the harlot. She was an outcast among outcasts, and as we will soon find out, she certainly had a reputation in this town. Or maybe she wasn't what she seemed at first glance. Either way, she was a very unlikely focus for one of the most significant occurrences and hottest-burning grassfires in human history. A grassfire that still burns brightly today.

How did it get started?

Once upon a time this woman was simply doing a daily chore. She walked to the outskirts of town to an old well to draw some water. There she noticed a man sitting by the well. Obviously, this man was not from her half-breed community. He was from the big city. So the fact that he was at the well was strange enough. But what happened next would prove to be even more disturbing.

This man spoke to her. He actually talked directly to her.

Even more odd, he asked her a question, as if she mattered.

"Will you give me a drink?" he asked.

The woman must have been shocked. Was he really speaking to her? She looked around to make sure there was no one else approaching the well. Sure enough, they were alone. What should she do?

"I am a half breed," she said. "How can you ask me for a drink?"

The man replied, "If you knew who it is who asks you for a drink, you would have asked him, and he would have given you living water."

The woman was even more perplexed. First he asked her for a drink. Now he was saying that she should have known to ask him for a drink when he didn't even have anything to draw water with! So she asked him, "How can you do this? You don't even have a bucket. Are you

greater than our forefather who built this well two thousand years ago?"

"Everyone who drinks of this water will be thirsty
again, but whoever drinks the water I give will never
thirst."

Never thirst again? She wondered if this man was simply
mocking her, but he continued: "Indeed, the water I give
will become a spring of water that gushes up life for ever
and ever!"

Now this was starting to get personal. Could this man
possibly know how dry and parched her life really was?
Could he know how hopeless she felt? Or was he simply
toying with her, like so many other men had done in the
past. She decided to call his bluff.

"Sir, give me this water, so that I will not get thirsty
and have to keep coming here to drink," she said. Even
though it broke all the social rules for them even to be talking, she probably wanted to end this charade. *Just give me
this special thirst-quenching water so I can go back to the town!*
she thought.

That's when it got really personal.

"Go and call your husband and bring him here," the
man said.

"I have no husband," she replied. Finally she thought
she was off the hook.

"You are right when you say you have no husband," he
said. "The truth is, you have had five husbands, and the
man you now have is not your husband. What you said is
quite true."

He called her bluff. Worse than that. It was as if he had
read the book of her life. Nonetheless, she continued to
evade his insight.

"You must be a prophet," she said. "Our fathers wor-
shipped here, but your people say we must worship in the
big city. Which is it?"

She tried desperately to change the subject from her personal life back to their cultural conflict. As painful as the cultural difference may have been, being a half breed was not personal. Having a man read the book of your most intimate secrets was personal.

But the man would not take the bait. "Neither place! It doesn't matter where you worship!" he explained, as if to say, "Pick a place, any place! Even right here!"

"What's more," he continued, "you don't have to reach some level of personal perfection to worship. In fact, true worshippers must worship out of the essence of who they are and in the reality of their lives—out of their spirits and in the truth of their lives. That is what is required."

Could it really be true? Was this man saying that the essence of who she was—a half breed—was good enough? And was it possible that the truth of her life—the reality of her pathetic existence—was a sufficient foundation for worshipping God? If both of these were true, then this woman's world would be turned upside down.

She had no idea that at that moment the entire world was changing. Up until that time, true worship of God was confined to a specific place in a specific city (the big city). True worship was relegated to the pure breeds who carefully followed very strict sanctions and procedures that would make them acceptable.

But there at that well outside the half-breed city in a conversation between two strangers—a man and a suspected harlot—the world was changing forever! Worship of God was about to expand to include all who would approach God out of the essence of who they are and in the reality of their lives.

All this woman had to do was open a door!

"I know that Messiah is coming," she said. "When he comes, he will explain everything to us." Can you hear the creaking of the hinge as she cracked open the door to her heart? She had been bruised and broken time and again, and now she could not quite get herself to believe. Only Messiah could overcome both her half-breed status and her heartbreaking life of sorrow and sin. "When he comes . . . ."

Turning directly to the woman, the man spoke in tones that were quite different from everything else he had said thus far. It was less a discussion and more a declaration, and it was focused entirely on the woman.

"I am He."

For the very first time, she looked up at this man. Their eyes met. In that moment, she knew that what he said was true. He was the Messiah. The door to an entirely new world had just opened, and her life as a half breed and a harlot had abruptly ended.

The spark had been lit! And the grassfire was about to spread across her town.

Just then, the man's friends returned to the well and were totally caught off guard to see him talking to a woman. If only they had known the rest of her story! But their concerns could not extinguish the spark. The woman quickly turned and headed back for the town, leaving behind the water jar. You see, her world had just been turned upside down, and the water she had come to draw was not so important now.

What was important was telling the people of her half-breed town, "Come, see a man who told me everything I ever did," which she did. The water mattered little. Her people mattered much.

Never forget that all great grassfires are ultimately about people. Your Grassfire Effect, as you recall, is the inevitable result of your expanding circle of influence. That influence always centers on people. We are about to see this woman's circle of influence expand in a dramatic way.

Put yourself in that community for a moment. A suspected harlot comes running from the well and claims to have met a man who knew everything she had ever done. How would the women in the community have reacted? Surely they would have wanted to find out the story once and for all on this woman, and thereby discover what the men of the community really were doing. And the men? They couldn't sit by idly and allow some stranger to expose their misdeeds! What did he know? Were the rumors true? Would they be exposed?

Or perhaps the townspeople just saw something different in her eyes. Maybe they could see that the shame was lifted and her countenance was brighter. Whatever the reason, they went with the woman toward the well.

Meanwhile, back at the well, the man's friends were confused. Their companion was caught alone with a half-breed woman. And now he was refusing to eat the lunch that he sent them to get. To make matters worse, he began speaking in riddles: "Do you not say, 'Four months more and then the harvest?' I tell you, open your eyes and look at the fields! They are ripe for harvest!"

I am told that this well, which is still there today, sits on an elevated piece of land that overlooks the town. Picture the scene. As he said the words, it is quite possible that the woman and the townspeople would have been in plain view, coming along the path that led from the town.

"Open your eyes": You are missing the spark that is igniting before you!

"Look at the fields": Look beyond water and food and see the heart of every grassfire—the people!

"They are ripe for harvest!": The Grassfire Effect is about to explode!

And so it did. As the story goes, many in that village met this man and discovered the new door that had been opened for them to God. This man who normally would not have even passed through this half-breed area decided to stay with them two more days to help encourage the grassfire that started in a most unlikely place with a most unlikely person.

Lessons from a Harlot's Grassfire

This woman's story has been told countless times across two millennia and is considered by many to be the definitive Christian teaching on what it really means to worship God. You can find the story in John 4. The man in the story is Jesus of Nazareth, a Jew. When Jesus and his disciples were passing through Samaria, they stopped at a well, and the disciples went to find some lunch. That is when this Samaritan woman approached. Samaritans were hated by the Jews because they were the product of Jews intermarrying with other cultures. But even worse, the Samaritans had adopted Jewish religious practices. Forbidden by the Jews to worship in Jerusalem, they set up their own temple on Mt. Gerizim. It was in this setting, at the base of Mt. Gerizim, that this most profound message on worship was delivered.

I wanted you to read this story without automatically thinking of it as a Bible story. It's far too easy to think of a story in the Bible as different from other stories. But this is very much a story about a half-breed woman who likely had a harlot's reputation. She was an outcast in an ethnic group of outcasts. She had little reason to think that her life would have any lasting impact. Yet she started a grassfire that has spanned generations. And her experience offers lessons for everyone who desires to see their life have meaning and purpose.

HARLOT GRASSFIRE LESSON NO. 1—
GRASSFIRES START WITH IDEAS

Remember where this book started? "All you need is one idea to change the world!" One spark. One idea. It took her awhile, but the woman at the well finally grasped the great idea Jesus was trying to communicate. A new door to God had been opened and she no longer had to fake it. What a profound concept. Instead of finding the right place to worship God and the right things to do to be accepted by God, all she had to do was open the door of her heart.

Could it be that simple? Yes. Quite often, the best grassfires are founded on the simplest of ideas. Remember Bill Gates? Not only did he see computers on everyone's desk; he saw that the computers would need brains (an operating system). He built the brains (software) and let others construct the body (hardware). Simple idea. No one else saw it.

HARLOT GRASSFIRE LESSON NO. 2—
GRASSFIRES ARE HARD TO EXPLAIN

Even though the best grassfires are based on simple ideas, at first they are difficult to describe. When I first developed the core concept of Grassfire, it would take me ten to twenty minutes just to explain how the referral system would work. Now the idea of online petitions needs little explanation.

In our story, Jesus patiently took this woman along a path of discussion before the idea clicked in her mind. He kept asking questions, probing, knowing that at best she was not getting the point and more likely evading his every inquiry. Jesus was patient. You will have to be patient as well.

HARLOT GRASSFIRE LESSON NO. 3— AT FIRST, FEW WILL BE IMPRESSED

When you light the first few sparks in the field, it will not look like much. At this point, the mayor will not give you the keys to the city. That's OK as long as you understand the Grassfire Effect. When the impact of your idea goes from igniting one person to two people, your Grassfire Effect impact will have increased a staggering 100 percent. When it goes from two to six people, your Grassfire Effect will have shot up 200 percent. Still, few will be impressed, but you should be.

Consider this woman at the well. If she had focused solely on how unimportant she was in the scope of life, she never would have run back to the village and invited others to meet Jesus. Fortunately, she stayed focused on the spark not the size of the flame.

That's what happened with Grassfire. That first week after our launch our total number of signers had grown to about 700 people out of 260 million Americans. I heard from some friends who said they "thought it would have been bigger by now." But what they didn't see was that the Grassfire Effect was well under way. In a short amount of time, the growth would be evident to all.

It is kind of like choosing between getting $10,000 today or getting a penny doubled for thirty days. Take the penny doubled. Here's why. After ten days of doubling the penny, you will only have $10.24, which is just one-tenth of 1 percent of $10,000. Sounds like a bad deal. On day 15, the penny will have grown to $327.68, which still pales in comparison to $10,000. But by day 20, the penny will have passed the $10,000 mark. When your penny doubles on day 30, you will be sitting on $10,737,418.24. That's right—almost $11 million! Which brings me to the fourth lesson.

HARLOT GRASSFIRE LESSON NO. 4—
PEOPLE WILL BE DRAWN TO YOUR GRASSFIRE

Once your penny turns into $10 million, you better believe that long-lost friends will suddenly come calling. That's because an expanding Grassfire Effect will bring more and more people in contact with your idea, invention, business, or organization. People will come.

The woman who came to the well could not have rallied anyone to do anything before she met Jesus. But then, with a spark in her heart, people were willing to follow her back to that well. People were drawn to her grassfire.

We tend to focus on this point—that people are drawn to grassfires. We like this. We like to give celebrity status in our society to those whose create grassfires. But as you get ready for your Grassfire Effect, always remember this: Attracting people is not the end game. People are always the end game.

Don't lose your focus. Remember what life here on earth is about? It's about people: your family, friends, neighbors—your circle of influence. If you desire a Grassfire Effect to fulfill your own selfish needs, that goal will eventually catch up to you. Yes, people will be drawn to an expanding grassfire. That's a good thing, as long as you keep your focus. Will you be able to handle your Grassfire Effect, or will it handle you? That will be decided by whether you can keep your focus.

HARLOT GRASSFIRE LESSON NO. 5—
WHEN THE FIRE SPREADS, REMEMBER LESSON NO. 1

Do you recall where we started this book? Grassfires always begin with ideas. All great movements, inventions, businesses, and individual accomplishments are birthed in ideas. But when the fire starts to spread, it's a challenge to remember the idea that started that first spark.

Before the fire starts to spread, it's easy to get discouraged because the spark seemed so revolutionary to us while others are slow to catch on. Then the fire spreads and we lose track of that first spark. That's why it is so crucial to solidify your core ideas during those early stages and never let go when the fire spreads.

The woman who brought her friends back to the well to meet Jesus never forgot that this grassfire was not really about her. She simply pointed the way. She remembered the big idea.

HARLOT GRASSFIRE LESSON NO. 6— TIMING IS EVERYTHING

Yes, your grassfire will spread. That is its nature. But you must remember that timing is everything. I can vividly recall many days at my nine-to-five job that made me feel like I was going nowhere. It would be Friday afternoon at 4:00 p.m. and I would get a call from a college friend who was heading for Europe. Then an e-mail would pop up from a buddy who was changing the world in Indonesia. Another close friend was living in the Alps, seeing the world. Yet another friend was completing his law degree and headed for a big job at a powerful firm.

What was I doing? I was writing marketing materials for a nonprofit organization. Sitting at a desk with four walls and no windows, I held a master's degree but was going nowhere professionally. To be honest, that office often felt more like a prison, a dead end.

But that wasn't the case at all. I didn't know it then, but I was honing the very skills that would help me fan those first Grassfire sparks into flame. Even more important, I was building the foundations for my marriage, learning how to be a dad to my two young daughters (I now have four daughters and a son), and digging deep footings of personal integrity and responsibility that would carry me throughout my life.

Consider the woman at the well. As noted earlier, we really do not know enough about her personal history to form solid opinions. She may not have been a harlot at all. She may have been unable to bear a child and as a result was cast off by several husbands. But look at what she did right. She was faithfully doing a simple chore: getting water. She understood her culture and customs enough to dialogue with Jesus. She even knew the prophecies of a Messiah who would change everything. Her life experiences prepared her for that spark. That is where most grassfires are birthed—in the ordinary course of your life, such as at your job. That is always the place to start.

HARLOT GRASSFIRE LESSON NO. 7—
YOUR FIRST SPARK WAS REALLY AN EMBER

One more lesson can be learned from this harlot's grassfire as you get ready to spark your own grassfire: Your grassfire didn't start with you! That spark of an idea in your mind really was an ember from a grassfire that was kindled long before you were born. There is a historical context to your life and your grassfire that can infuse meaning and purpose into everything you do.

Consider our story of the woman at the well. During one of her evasions, the woman mentioned that the well actually dated back to a spiritual forefather of both Jews and Samaritans. She said to Jesus: "You aren't greater than our father Jacob, are you? He gave us the well and drank from it himself, as did his sons and livestock" (John 4:12).

I would offer to you that as she posed that question Jesus may have chuckled a bit to himself. That's because he knew what happened seventeen hundred or so years earlier on that exact spot of ground where he was sitting.

When you have time, read in Genesis the story of the great patriarchs of the Jewish faith: Abraham, his son Isaac, and his grandson Jacob. I'll pick up the story with Jacob, who was called the "supplanter" because he was always plotting, scheming, brokering deals, looking for a way out. Jacob actually stole his father's blessing that was reserved for his older brother, Esau. That's who Jacob was by his very nature—a conniver.

The turning point in Jacob's life came at a place called Peniel, when God himself came and met Jacob. Not only did God meet Jacob; he wrestled with him, left him wounded, and changed his name to "Israel," which means "he struggles with God." (Remember how important names are?)

The next morning, Jacob woke up and saw his bitter brother Esau on the horizon. It was a good bet that when Esau found Jacob he would try to kill him. Conniving Jacob deserved no better. Jacob's heart must have been pounding. But instead of looking for a sneaky way out like he had always done in the past, he went ahead of his family and bowed down before his brother. And instead of the worst happening, "Esau ran to meet him, hugged him, threw his arms around him, and kissed him" (Gen. 33:4).

Jacob then turned to his brother and said, "If I have found favor with you, take this gift from my hand. For indeed, I have seen your face, [and it is like] seeing God's face, since you have accepted me" (Gen. 33:10). What a change from the conniving Jacob! The night before, Jacob had actually seen the face of God. Now, in his own brother, he again saw God's face. No longer were people pawns in Jacob's manipulative game. Jacob had seen the face of God, and it changed the way he saw people. This is the core result of an encounter with God: a changed heart that leads to a changed view of life, that leads to changed actions.

The Bible makes this clear. Want to fulfill God's commandments? Love your neighbor. Want to show God that you love him? Love your brother. Love is the fulfillment of the law; loving others is the proof that you love God. You can't love God without loving others. Why? Just ask Jacob. When you have an encounter with God and his love, it transforms the way you see people.

Jacob's Altar and Jacob's Well

But Jacob's journey doesn't end there. After he and his brother parted ways, Jacob and his family went to another region, called Shechem. There he bought a piece of land and set up an altar. What's significant about this? Two things. First of all, this is the first time that Jacob ever built an altar to God. Jacob had previously set up pillars, stones, and other tributes but no altars. Prior to this moment, the Bible never mentions Jacob building an altar. That's because Jacob was usually brokering a deal, working a plan, and leveraging his resources . . . even with God. The pillars and stones and tributes he established sure sounded good, but there was something missing at the very core — the actions were still about Jacob.

But outside Shechem, after wrestling with God and seeing God's grace in his brother's eyes, he set up an altar he named "El Elohe Israel," which means "God, the God of Israel." This altar's name had a very important meaning for this former conniver. Today when we think of "Israel," we think of the nation in the Middle East. But when Jacob built this altar, there was no nation of Israel. In fact, there were no people of Israel. Jacob *was* Israel. That was *his* name.

So when Jacob proclaimed, "El Elohe Israel," he was really saying, "God, the God of *me!*" Finally, after much wrestling, Jacob was ready to worship. So he built an altar. *God, the God of me!* He finally had personalized his relationship with God.

It gives me goose bumps to think about that moment in Jacob's life when his entire world changed, and, as a result, all of human history was forever changed. Did Jacob know that his actions were channeling the course of human history? I doubt it. This was personal. This was about wrestling with God—meeting God face-to-face. This was about discovering how to see people; to see God's face in their faces. And most important, this was about discovering what it really meant to worship God—God the God of me!

I remember vividly the day I built that altar and proclaimed, "God the God of Steve!" It was the greatest day in my life, and there is a connection between my encounter and Jacob's experience. A direct connection.

That's because Jacob did something else. . . .

He dug a well!

That same well where the half-breed woman was drawing water when she met the Man who told her everything she ever wanted to know. That same well where Jesus gave the world a picture for all the ages of how men should worship God—out of the essence of who they are (in spirit) and in the reality of their lives (in truth). That same spot where the greatest teaching on worship was ever delivered. It took place precisely where Jacob had first discovered true worship some seventeen hundred years before. Could that possibly be a coincidence? Could the one who said, "Before Abraham (and therefore Isaac and Jacob) was, I am" (John 8:58), have possibly not known what had happened in that place?

When Jacob dug that well, he lit a grassfire. That fire burned brightly enough that Jacob's experience of wrestling with God and building that altar and digging that well were passed down from generation to generation. But seventeen hundred years later, those roaring flames of Jacob's grassfire were not burning quite so brightly. In fact, a few of those original embers from that fire had just been smoldering for all these years, hardly noticed by anyone.

Those embers would smolder until Jesus and a half-breed woman met at that same exact spot. Those embers Jacob had kindled so many generations before would be lit again in the heart of a suspected harlot.

It was a grassfire that was seventeen hundred years in the making. Today, whenever that encounter between Jesus and the harlot is discussed—dare I say thousands of times every day?—Jacob's spark is rekindled again. Each time another person discovers they can worship God out of the essence of who they are and in the reality of their lives (instead of out of some dead ritual or self-striving), they really are building that altar and proclaiming "God the God of me!" Jacob's grassfire is fanned into flame once again.

But don't think for a minute that the lineage of your grassfire is any shorter. The sparks of your life have deep roots that go back generations. Perhaps a few of those roots are coming to mind right now as you read these words. Keep those sparks (i.e., those people) in your mind so you can recall them when you face tough times. If you are having trouble finding that generational link, keep looking. It is there.

Just as your life's sparks have deep roots in the past, the grassfires you start are intended to reach forward for generations. So often we focus on the bad in our world: sin, destruction, hate. Even people of faith often quote the Bible passage that indicates that a father's sins will be visited on his children to the third and fourth generations. But there is a much greater force in this world. Good is greater than evil! Faith is greater than unbelief! Blessings are more powerful than curses! The Bible says blessings extend not only to two or three generations, but go for a thousand generations. That's longer than all of recorded human history. And it means your grassfires will continue long after your children's children's children are burying their children. Think about that!

You are not an island. Your impact will touch people who are yet to be born. Do you believe it? You should. It's the Grassfire Effect at work: the inevitable result of your expanding circle of influence.

Once upon a time a person unique in all of human history was conceived and several months later that person was born. That person's life and experience was distinct from any that had gone before or would ever come. That person's life was more fascinating than any legend or fairy tale because that person's life was real. And that person is you.

Scientists tell us that the sound waves created by your first cry when you were born are still traveling out into space. Is it so hard to imagine that the effort and effect of your life will extend out as well? Even if some of your grassfires lay dormant for hundreds of years as overlooked embers, don't despair. Keep on sparking. The world will change. *Your* world will change. It simply must.

Looking for more ways
to increase your Grassfire Effect?

Visit GrassfireEffect.com
to post your comments, access additional
resources, and sign up for Steve Elliott's
motivational e-mail update, "The Spark."

GrassfireEffect.com